The Untapped Power of Family:

Building Family Capital

Apostle Tommy E. Quick

Opening Prayer

O Creator of life, the Ancient of days,
We lift our hearts in reverent praise.
To You, the Architect, divine and wise,
Who forms each bond that never dies.

Bless this family, Your chosen design,
A sacred thread in Your eternal line.
Grant us vision to see the untold worth,
In the daily rhythms of life on this earth.

Let love be the seed, faith the strong vine,
In the soil of purpose, let our roots intertwine.
In laughter, in sorrow, in trials, in cheer,
Reveal the unseen, Your presence so near.

Awaken our hearts to potential untamed,
To live for Your glory, our purpose proclaimed.
Through the mundane, may Your beauty arise,
A masterpiece woven, to bless and inspire.

Grant us the courage to build and to grow,
To strengthen the bonds that Your wisdom bestows.
For every moment, small or grand,
Is held in the palm of Your sovereign hand.

O Lord, the Builder of nations and kin,
Guide us in grace to draw others in.
For families united in love and in light,
Will shine as beacons in the world's darkest night.

So we ask in this prayer, with hearts full of zeal,
Make us stewards of this treasure so real.
May this book be a seed, a lamp, a flame,
To bring honor and glory to Your holy name.
Amen.

by Apostle Tommy E. Quick

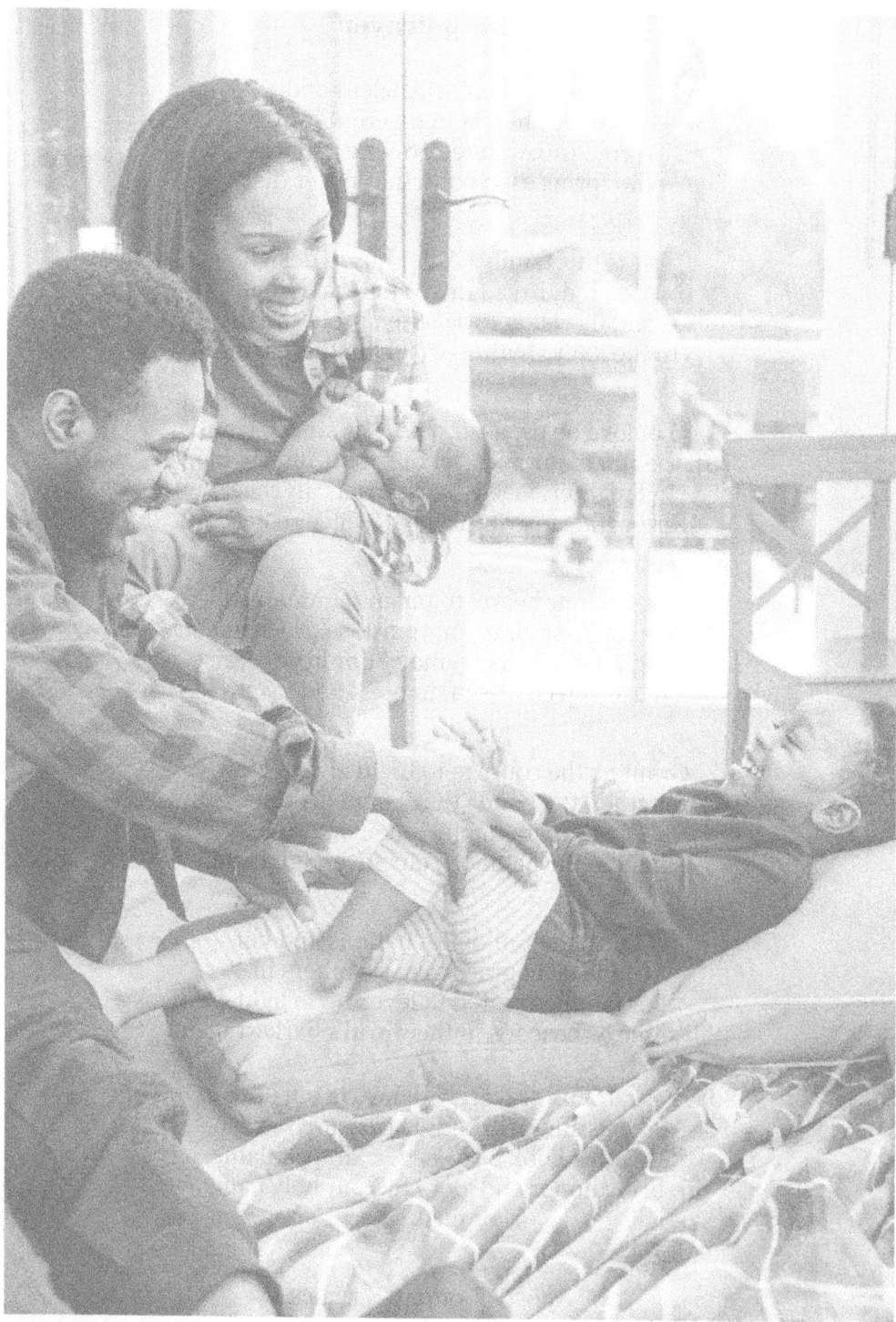

Table of Contents

Introduction

What if the choices we make today about our families ripple through generations, shaping the destiny of our children and grandchildren? What if the erosion of family values, which now feels like a distant cultural trend, is actually a threat sitting at your doorstep—one that could profoundly affect the flourishing of your own household?

This isn't just an abstract societal issue; it is a deeply personal one. The stakes are too high to ignore, for it is within the family that the seeds of faith, resilience, and love are planted—or lost.

Our culture is quick to celebrate individual potential, offering countless pathways to personal happiness and self-fulfilment. But how often do we stop to ask: at what cost? Behind the pursuit of independence lies a stark reality—families are breaking down, children are suffering, and generations are losing the spiritual inheritance that only strong, biblically grounded families can provide.

For nearly five decades, I have stood before congregations, counselling, preaching, and challenging families to rise to the potential God has placed within them. As a husband of 39 years to my beloved Valerie, a father to five wonderful children, and a grandfather to many more, I have learned one irrefutable truth: the family is one of God's greatest gifts to humanity. Yet, I've also observed how often its divine power goes untapped.

Families struggle, drift apart, and sometimes even collapse under the weight of challenges they were never meant to face alone.

1

I want to begin by asking you a question: Have you ever considered if there lies untapped power within you a wealth that is made accessible as we endeavor to live out God's family love plan? If so, have you considered how to reach this untapped capital. I call it capital because it is indeed a medium of exchange. God honors it and God rewards it in ways that most will never experience because of their refusal to live according to God's love plan for the family. They fail to tap into it, but you can learn to.

I encourage you to read this book thoroughly and methodically apply its principles. I'm not speaking of financial riches or material possessions only; I'm talking about something far greater—*family capital*. This is the wealth of love, faith, unity, and shared purpose that God designs to guard the lives and hearts of each family so we may experience the joy He has planned for our lives. Over the years, I've seen families unlock this capital and transform not only their homes breaking through generational curses of brokenness and poverty and become blessings to their communities.

As parents, children, and members of this culture, we cannot stand idly by. The family is God's chosen vessel for human flourishing, and its defense is a sacred responsibility.

PART I: Families Under-siege

Chapter 1: The Urgency of the Moment

Consider the sobering truth: nearly half of all first marriages in the United States end in divorce. This is not just a statistic; it is a heartbreak that is felt in the lives of parents and children alike. The pain of divorce extends beyond the moment of separation, leaving children to endure feelings of instability and loss. For many, the scars last a lifetime, affecting their future relationships and their view of God's love and faithfulness.

What about your family? Are you guarding your marriage against the forces that pull so many apart—infidelity, financial stress, and a lack of commitment? The fight for your family's future begins with recognizing the sacredness of the covenant God designed marriage to be. Imagine the legacy you could leave if, instead of succumbing to the cultural norm, you stood firm in God's truth, modeling sacrificial love for your children to see and replicate.

The Fatherhood Crisis—America's Silent Epidemic

For decades, families have served as the bedrock of strong communities, passing down values, faith, and a sense of responsibility from one generation to the next. Yet, today, we are witnessing a devastating crisis—one that threatens to erode the very foundation of our society. It is a crisis that does not make headlines in the way economic downturns or political scandals do, yet its consequences are far more enduring. It is the fatherhood crisis, a silent epidemic that has left millions of children without the steady hand of a father to guide them.

The Root of the Crisis: Policies That Undermined Fathers

Many attribute the disintegration of the family, particularly in Black communities, to systemic racism or economic disparity. However, a deeper examination reveals that the single most destructive force against the family has been the unintended consequences of welfare policies introduced in the 1960s. Specifically, the Aid to Families with Dependent Children (AFDC) program, part of President Lyndon B. Johnson's "Great Society" initiative, incentivized fatherless homes by providing financial assistance to unmarried mothers while discouraging marriage.

For the first time in American history, the federal government financially rewarded the absence of fathers. The results were catastrophic. In 1950, only 17% of Black children were born to unmarried mothers. By 2010, that number had soared to 72%. This was not an organic shift in cultural values but a calculated shift in behavior—a direct response to the financial incentives created by welfare expansion. What government funds, it multiplies.

The tragic irony is that before these policies, the Black family was among the strongest in America. More than 80% of Black households were two-parent homes before 1970. Faith, family, and education were the cornerstones of the Black community. But as government programs expanded, fathers were subtly and systematically pushed out of the home. Communities once rich in stability and structure saw their cultural norms upended, leading to a host of social crises—poverty, crime, educational decline, and generational cycles of dependency.

The Devastating Impact of Fatherlessness

The absence of fathers has left a gaping wound in our society. Countless studies affirm that children who grow up without a father are:

- Four times more likely to live in poverty
- More likely to drop out of school
- More likely to engage in criminal behavior and be incarcerated
- At higher risk for teenage pregnancy and single parenthood themselves

God designed the family with purpose and order. Fathers provide identity, stability, and discipline. The absence of a father leaves a child searching for validation in all the wrong places. When fathers fail to fulfill their divine role, the enemy eagerly steps in to redefine masculinity, distort identity, and enslave young men to destructive lifestyles.

Progressive Ideologies & The Attack on the Family

In recent years, progressive ideologies such as Critical Race Theory (CRT) and radical gender politics have compounded the crisis, promoting an anti-nuclear family agenda under the guise of equity and social justice. CRT proponents argue that "family privilege" is an unfair advantage, much like "white privilege." One CRT source states, "Like White privilege, family privilege is an unacknowledged and unearned benefit."

But what they call privilege, God calls *design*.

CRT and identity politics seek to divide families rather than strengthen them. By labeling traditional family structures as tools of oppression, these ideologies drive a wedge between generations and encourage dependency on the state rather than reliance on God and family. Instead of lifting people up, they train them to see themselves as perpetual victims.

Alternative Structures, Same Challenges

The rise of single-parent homes, cohabitating couples, and blended families presents new complexities. Perhaps you see this in your own family or your circle of friends. These structures often struggle to provide the stability and security children need to thrive, despite the best intentions of those involved. Yet God's design for the family—a covenant union between one man and one woman, rooted in faith—is not simply an ideal; it is the blueprint for generational flourishing.

This is not to dismiss the courage of single parents or the unique dynamics of blended families. Rather, it is to affirm that we can—and must—strive to align our lives with God's purpose. Are you equipping your family to grow in faith and resilience, even amid cultural headwinds? What would it look like to recommit to God's design, whatever your starting point?

The Cultural War on Marriage

Marriage, once a cornerstone of adulthood, has been rebranded as optional, even burdensome. Perhaps you've felt the pressure yourself—the cultural voice whispering that career, personal fulfillment, or freedom is more important than family. But the truth is that this shift has left many feeling isolated and unfulfilled as they get older without a life-long partner and strong united family.

God created marriage not as a burden, but as a blessing—a picture of Christ's love for the Church and a foundation for a thriving household.

If you are married, consider how your union reflects God's covenantal love. If you are single, how are you preparing yourself for the sacred responsibility of marriage? By treating marriage as a divine calling rather than a social convenience, you can reclaim its sacredness and pass that understanding to the next generation.

Sexual Ethics and Identity: A Call to Truth

Our culture's departure from biblical sexual ethics is not a harmless evolution; it is a direct assault on the foundation of family. Premarital sex, pornography, and casual relationships are normalized, leaving individuals—and their families— spiritually depleted and emotionally fragmented. Even children, exposed to these values through media and peers, are at risk of losing their understanding of God's design for love and commitment.

As parents and leaders, how are we equipping our children to stand firm in truth? Are we modeling purity, faithfulness, and integrity in our own lives? And how are we addressing the growing confusion around gender and identity with both compassion and conviction? To build a family that honors God, we must confront these cultural lies with the truth of Scripture.

The Spiritual Crisis in the Home

Perhaps the greatest threat to the family is not external but internal—a spiritual complacency that leaves families vulnerable to the world's lies. Fewer families attend church together, pray together, or center their lives on Scripture.

Without these anchors, how can we expect our children to withstand the storm of secular values unscathed?

Take a moment to reflect: Is your family firmly rooted in Christ? Are you prioritizing prayer, worship, and biblical teaching in your home?

The responsibility to build spiritual family capital begins with you. By reclaiming God's design for the family, you can pass on a legacy of faith, hope, and love that will outlast cultural trends and stand the test of time.

Restoring Fatherhood & Strengthening Families

The solution to this crisis is not found in more government programs or cultural blame-shifting. It is found in a return to God's original blueprint for the family—one where fathers lead, mothers nurture, and children are raised in a covenant of love and discipline.

Biblical Principles for Rebuilding the Family

1. **Marriage Before Children**
   - God's design is clear: marriage is the foundation for raising children. Studies show that marriage before children correlates directly with prosperity and stability.
   - "Whoso findeth a wife findeth a good thing, and obtaineth favour of the Lord." (Proverbs 18:22, KJV)
   - "He who finds a [true and faithful] wife finds a good thing and obtains favor and approval from the Lord." (Proverbs 18:22, AMPC)

2. **Spiritual & Moral Leadership of Fathers**
   - Fathers must reclaim their God-given role as leaders, protectors, and providers in the home.
   - "Train up a child in the way he should go: and when he is old, he will not depart from it." (Proverbs 22:6, KJV)

- "Train up a child in the way he should go [teaching him to seek God's wisdom and will for his abilities and talents], even when he is old he will not depart from it." (Proverbs 22:6, AMPC)

3. **Faith-Based Family Counseling & Mentorship**

   - The restoration of families begins in churches and faith-based organizations. Programs that disciple young men, encourage marriage, and equip parents with biblical parenting skills are critical.

4. **Educational & Economic Empowerment**

   - Teaching family's financial literacy, entrepreneurship, and biblical stewardship strengthens generational wealth and reduces dependency on government aid.

   - "A good man leaveth an inheritance to his children's children: and the wealth of the sinner is laid up for the just." (Proverbs 13:22, KJV)

   - "A good man leaves an inheritance [of moral stability and goodness] to his children's children, And the wealth of the sinner is stored up for [the hands of] the righteous." (Proverbs 13:22, AMPC)

The Path Forward

If we are to see a revival in the family, we must reject the lies that have enslaved generations and boldly proclaim God's truth. The family is God's first institution, and His design is not outdated—it is eternal.

The fatherhood crisis may be America's silent epidemic, but the solution is loud and clear: Return to God. Return to family. Return to His perfect plan.

Your Call to Action

The cultural trends threatening the family are powerful, but they are not insurmountable. As believers, we are called to be salt and light—to push back against darkness and to stand firm on God's truth. The family is worth fighting for—not only for your own sake but for the generations yet to come.

What will you do today to strengthen your family? Will you commit to prayer, intentional time together, or a deeper engagement with God's Word? Will you model Christ-like love, even when it requires sacrifice? The choices you make now can transform your family into a beacon of hope and resilience in a world desperately in need of both.

The defense of the family begins with you. Let this be your moment to stand in the gap, to reclaim the beauty of God's design, and to leave a legacy of faith that will endure for generations.

Why Defending the Family Matters Now More Than Ever

We must acknowledge, families are struggling more than ever. Relationships are breaking down, and communities are crumbling because the foundation of strong family structures has weakened. Divorce rates remain high, fatherlessness is a tragic norm, and marriage is often viewed as a temporary arrangement rather than a sacred, lifelong promise.

These shifts have created a breach in the very fabric of society, leaving children and adults alike vulnerable to a host of challenges that extend far beyond the home.

Too many children today are growing up without the role models, stability, and love they need to thrive. Without the guidance of a Christ-centered family, souls are left vulnerable to an identity crisis that leads to depression, low self-esteem, and hopelessness. These wounds often manifest in cycles of educational failure, substance abuse, incarceration, and immorality. The instability that begins in broken homes ripples outward, creating hurting souls who, in their pain, often hurt others.

This crisis is not just a personal issue—it is a societal one. When families fail to provide the spiritual, emotional, and relational support God designed them to give, the consequences are devastating. Communities lose their anchor, children lose their direction, and generations lose the hope and resilience needed to build a flourishing future.

We must not despair but act, there is hope. The family was God's idea, and His design has not failed—it has been abandoned. By returning to biblical principles and reclaiming God's purpose for marriage, parenting, and relationships, families can once again become the safe havens and beacons of hope they were always meant to be.

The time to act is now. The stakes are high, but the rewards of building Christ-empowered families are eternal. Together, we can restore the broken foundations, heal wounded souls, and pass on a legacy of faith, strength, and love to the generations yet to come.

The Urgency of Building Family Capital

We stand at a crossroads and the survival of the family as a God-ordained institution is at stake. Modern trends have shaken the foundation of families, leaving broken relationships, fractured communities, and generations struggling to find their way. Divorce rates remain unacceptably high, fatherlessness has become tragically common, and many no longer view marriage as a covenant for life. These changes have created a societal breach where children lack the stability and role models they desperately need, leading to devastating consequences: loss of personal identity, depression, low self-esteem, hopelessness, educational failure, addiction, incarceration, and even cycles of generational pain.

This is where Family Capital offers hope. Families grounded in God's principles and united by shared values and purpose have the power to reverse these trends. Family capital refers to the spiritual, emotional, relational, and intellectual resources that families intentionally create and pass down to future generations. It is the strength that enables families not only to endure but to thrive in the face of cultural pressures.

To heal our society, we must start at the root: rebuilding the family. Families built on God's design become places where faith, character, and purpose are cultivated, transforming not only individual lives but entire communities.

What Families with Strong Family Capital Provide

Families rich in family capital act as anchors of stability, hope, and resilience, offering:

- **Spiritual Heritage**: Teaching faith in God and following biblical principles equips families with wisdom and guidance for navigating life's challenges. This foundation creates a legacy of faith passed down through generations.

- **Emotional Resilience**: In a world of uncertainty, families grounded in love and forgiveness provide a safe haven where members feel supported and valued. Emotional resilience nurtured at home strengthens individuals to face life's struggles with grace.

- **Relational Wealth**: Strong families cultivate deep, meaningful relatives within the family and beyond. These relationships become the framework for empathy, association, and neighborhood strengthening

- **Practical Wisdom**: Teaching life skills such as financial stewardship, effective communication, and conflict resolution equips families to thrive in the practical realities of life.

When families fail to build this kind of capital, the effects ripple far beyond the home. Schools, workplaces, governments, and even churches feel the impact of broken homes and lost potential. This decline continually weakens the moral and spiritual fabric of our society, leaving communities vulnerable to instability and decay.

Family Capital: True Riches and God's Promises

However, family capital is more than an earthly resource; it holds eternal significance. Jesus referred to intangible blessings as "true riches" in Scripture (Luke 16:11). These riches, rooted in God's promises and covenants, are the ultimate rewards for families who align themselves with His design.

God created families to play a vital role in His eternal plan—to populate the earth, glorify His name, and serve as the foundation of human flourishing. The command to "be fruitful and multiply and replenish the earth" (Genesis 1:28) has not been revoked. Families remain central to God's plan to reflect His glory and build His kingdom.

God's Promises and Covenants Through Family Capital

Throughout Scripture, God has made promises to families that align themselves with His purposes. These covenants illustrate how family capital becomes the gateway to spiritual and generational blessings.

1. **The Covenant of Blessing with Abraham's Family**

   - *Scriptural Basis*: Genesis 12:2-3
     God promised Abraham that through his family, "all the families of the earth will be blessed." Abraham's faith and obedience established a generational covenant that culminated in the coming of Jesus Christ.

   - **Connection to Family Capital**: Abraham's family nurtured a spiritual heritage, teaching faith, obedience, and trust in God's promises. Families today can similarly position themselves to receive generational blessings by cultivating faith-centered homes.

2. **Noah's Covenant of Preservation**

   - *Scriptural Basis*: Genesis 9:9-17
     Noah's obedience and the unity of his family resulted in God's covenant of preservation, symbolized by the rainbow.

   - **Connection to Family Capital**: Noah's family exemplified relational wealth and emotional resilience as they worked together to fulfill God's instructions. Their unity preserved humanity and God's glory on earth.

3. **The Davidic Covenant: A Legacy of Leadership**

   o *Scriptural Basis*: 2 Samuel 7:12-16
   God promised David that his house and kingdom
   would endure forever, a promise fulfilled through Jesus
   Christ.

   o **Connection to Family Capital**: Families that
   invest in legacy-building through faith, wisdom, and
   strong relationships position themselves for
   generational influence and leadership.

4. **The New Covenant in Christ**

   o *Scriptural Basis*: Luke 22:20; Hebrews 8:10
   The ultimate covenant is through Jesus Christ,
   offering salvation and eternal life to all who
   believe.

   o **Connection to Family Capital**: Families grounded
   in the New Covenant prioritize faith and pass down
   the gospel message, creating a ripple effect that
   advances God's kingdom.

The Undiminished Role of Families in God's Plan

Despite cultural shifts, God's design for the family remains
unchanged. Families are called to:

1. **Reflect His Glory**: By living according to His Word and
   demonstrating His love, families reveal God's character to the
   world.

2. **Raise Godly Generations**: Intentional parenting and
   discipleship equip children to carry forward God's mission.

3. **Build His Kingdom**: Families serve as the bedrock of
   churches, communities, and societies that honor God.

When families align with God's purposes, they become instruments of His glory, advancing His eternal mission to fill the earth with His presence.

True Riches: Eternal Rewards for Faithful Families

Families that intentionally build family capital receive blessings that extend beyond the present. These include:

- **God's Favor**: Families walking in obedience experience His provision, protection, and presence.

- **Generational Blessings**: The faithfulness of one generation sets the stage for blessings upon the next (Proverbs 13:22).

- **Eternal Impact**: Families aligned with God's will leave a legacy that influences countless lives for Christ.

The time to reclaim the family's God-given role as the foundation of society is now. Will you become a family champion? This book equips you with the tools to grow your family capital, strengthen your home, and align your family with God's design. Together, we can reverse the decline, heal brokenness, and build families that thrive—not just for themselves but for future generations.

By putting God first and intentionally building family capital, we can restore hope to a broken world. The choice to invest in strong families is not just about survival—it's about leaving a legacy of faith, love, and purpose for generations to come. Let's take the first step together.

Chapter 2: Understanding Family Capital

Unlocking the Power of Family Capital

In the face of family fragmentation and moral decline, the family stands as God's primary institution for nurturing life, character, and legacy. Yet, the power of the family remains untapped in our generation, threatening the stability of future generations unless we intentionally return to Judeo-Christian values. At the heart of this restoration lies *Family Capital*, the collective reservoir of spiritual, emotional, social, and intellectual resources that families generate, sustain, and pass down across generations.

Family Capital is not merely a private asset but a dynamic and transformative force that shapes individuals, strengthens communities, and preserves cultures. Each family member's unique contributions—faith, love, knowledge, skills, and traditions—amplify the family's overall strength and resilience.

Families with strong capital not only thrive internally but also serve as the foundational building blocks of society. In this chapter, we explore what *Family Capital* entails, its vital components, and how CFADD's mission equips families to build this enduring wealth.

What Is Family Capital?

Family Capital encompasses the interconnected resources that families generate to sustain faith, promote values, and cultivate responsible, morally grounded individuals. It includes:

- **Spiritual Resources**: Teaching and modeling devotion to and faith in God, instilling biblical principles, and shaping a family's worldview and decision-making. Spiritual capital is the root of resilience and moral direction.

- **Emotional Bonds and Resilience**: Through love, trust, and shared experiences, families build a network of empathy and security that strengthens each member's ability to face adversity.

- **Social Capital and Legacy**: Families pass down customs, traditions, and relational skills that equip younger generations to engage effectively in society and carry forward a legacy of integrity and service.

- **Intellectual and Educational Resources**: Families foster critical thinking, skills development, and a love of learning, helping children grow into well-rounded individuals who positively contribute to society.

This multifaceted wealth creates a robust system where spiritual values, emotional strength, strong relations, and intellectual growth enhance one another, forming an enduring legacy that far surpasses material gain.

Family Capital is A Force for Social Stability

Strong families are the bedrock of stable communities and flourishing societies. The breakdown of family structures weakens the social fabric, leaving individuals vulnerable and communities fragmented. Families with *Family Capital*, however, build stability by:

- **Sustaining Faith**: Families grounded in God's Word create a spiritual heritage that shapes values and decision- making across generations.

- **Promoting Emotional Resilience**: A strong family network provides the safety and encouragement needed to face life's challenges with confidence.

- **Fostering Social Responsibility**: Families teach relational skills, fostering integrity, cooperation, and service to others.

- **Equipping Future Generations**: By prioritizing education and mentorship, families empower their children to thrive in life and contribute to the common good.

Through CFADD's initiatives, such as *Just Parents, Dad's at Duty,* and *The Marriage Builders Project*, and others, families are equipped to cultivate these resources intentionally, ensuring their capital grows and multiplies across generations.

Family Capital in Practice: High-Aperture Perspectives

To fully grasp the transformative power of *Family Capital*, we must examine it through a high-magnification lens, focusing on specific areas of family life that contribute to its growth:

- **Spiritual Foundation**

  Faith is the cornerstone of *Family Capital*. Families that intentionally teach and model biblical principles create a legacy of spiritual resilience. As Deuteronomy 6:6-7 instructs, parents must diligently teach their children God's Word, shaping their worldview and moral compass. CFADD's *Just Parents* program equips families to make faith central, ensuring their legacy extends beyond the immediate generation.

- **The Role of Fathers in Breaking Poverty Cycles**

  Research and scripture affirm the generational benefits of father involvement. Proverbs 13:22 states, "A good man leaves an inheritance to his children's children." Fathers who are present and engaged reduce poverty cycles, improve academic outcomes, and lower criminal behavior among youth. CFADD's *Dad's at Duty* program fosters father-child relationships, directly impacting families and addressing broader societal challenges.

- **Emotional and Social Wealth**

  Healthy families nurture emotional bonds and relational skills that build trust, empathy, and cooperation. CFADD's *Marriage Builders Project* promotes commitment and mutual respect, modeling healthy male-female relationships for children. Families that cultivate emotional security pass these qualities to the next generation, creating a ripple effect of relational health.

- **A Legacy of Faith and Integrity**

  Proverbs 24:3-4 reminds us that "through wisdom is a house builded; and by understanding it is established." Families that prioritize spiritual and relational tools leave a godly inheritance of responsibility, honesty, and diligence. CFADD encourages families to view their legacy not just in terms of material wealth but as a foundation of wisdom and faith.

Family Capital and Quantum Principles

The principles of quantum theory provides a powerful analogy for understanding the dynamics of *Family Capital*. Consider these parallels:

- **Quantum Interconnectedness: Family Unity**

  In quantum physics, particles are interconnected in ways that defy classical understanding. Similarly, family members are deeply connected; the decisions, values, and behaviors of one member ripple throughout the family, influencing its collective identity. Parents who model integrity, faith, and resilience create a network of support and unity that strengthens the entire family.

- **Quantum Potential: Family Influence**

  Quantum theory suggests that particles exist in multiple potential states until they are observed. Likewise, family members hold untapped potential that can be realized through supportive relationships and purposeful parenting. Families that nurture each person's God-given abilities transform individual strengths into a powerful collective legacy.

- **Quantum Synergy: The Whole Is Greater Than the Sum**

  Quantum systems exhibit behaviors collectively that are impossible in isolation. This synergy is mirrored in families where shared values and mutual support amplify their impact. *Family Capital* thrives when family members unite in purpose, achieving more together than they could alone.

- **Quantum "Observation": Intentional Parenting**

  In quantum mechanics, observation affects reality. Similarly, parents who intentionally "observe" their children—encouraging their strengths and guiding their growth—play a transformative role in shaping their character and destiny.

- **Quantum Tunneling: Overcoming Challenges**

  Quantum tunneling allows particles to pass through barriers that seem insurmountable. Families with strong capital—faith, support, and resilience—can overcome generational obstacles such as poverty, addiction, or broken relationships, emerging stronger on the other side.

The erosion of Judeo-Christian values has left *Family Capital* at risk, threatening not only individual families but the stability of society itself. The time to act is now. Each family must reclaim its God-given role as the cornerstone of faith, resilience, and legacy.

Family Capital's Dynamic, Transformative Force

Family Capital is not a static resource; it is a dynamic, transformative force that grows through intentional effort and faithful stewardship. Through CFADD's programs and teachings, families are empowered to build this capital with purpose, creating a foundation that not only endures but transforms lives and communities. By aligning with Judeo- Christian values, families can unlock the untapped power of *Family Capital*, blessing future generations and glorifying God.

The stability of a family grounded in God's law reflects the steadfastness of the Lord's preservation. When divine law is neglected, families falter, and individuals become "like waves of the sea, tossed and driven" (James 1:6, KJV). Such instability fosters confusion, aimlessness, and a loss of moral clarity, leaving lives fragmented and susceptible to external influences.

A God-centered family acts as an anchor in the tumult of life. It nurtures spiritual resilience, emotional strength, and moral direction. Just as the Lord preserved the souls of Noah and his family during the flood through their obedience and unity, so too does He preserve families who remain rooted in His Word (Genesis 6–9).

Families that reject divine order often succumb to shifting cultural winds, unable to discern truth from falsehood. Without God as their foundation, they lose the ability to transmit enduring values and principles. The absence of spiritual heritage deprives future generations of the faith and devotion necessary to navigate life's challenges. Joshua's declaration, "As for me and my house, we will serve the Lord" (Joshua 24:15, KJV), underscores the importance of a family's commitment to God's principles.

Moreover, the loss of moral clarity results in fractured relationships, weakened communities, and a diminished capacity to impart wisdom and hope. This spiritual legacy underscores the profound impact a family can have when aligned with God's will.

To neglect divine law is to abandon the soul's preservation. By embracing God's plan, families can become the steadfast lights needed to restore moral clarity, strength, and purpose to a world adrift. Let us, therefore, commit to building homes anchored in God's unchanging truth.

Family capital, as I define it, is the spiritual and emotional wealth that comes from their relationships, faith, and shared values within a family. Family capital ensures human flourishing and creates an enduring legacy that impacts generations. It is what sustains families through hardships, builds resilience, and creates a foundation for success—not by the world's standards but by God's.

However, strong families rich in the love of God, don't just help their own family members—they benefit society as a whole. Families with *Family Capital* raise children who are responsible, morally grounded, and prepared to make a positive impact. These families also strengthen their neighborhoods, schools, and communities by promoting stability, trust, and shared values.

God ordained families as the building blocks of a healthy society. That's why our programs—like *Just Parents, Dad's at Duty,* and *The Marriage Builders Project, our Online Family University among others*—help families build *Family Capital* intentionally. By strengthening faith, creating strong relationships, and passing down values, families will be resilient (overcoming all challenges to their love and unity).

This book was born out of countless counseling sessions and sermons where I witnessed the same patterns: families desperate for answers, unaware of the resources God had already placed within their grasp. I've seen families find healing when they embraced the principles of love, forgiveness, and faith. I've seen fathers step into their God-given roles, mothers rebuild bridges of connection, and children rediscover the strength of their heritage.

When families focus on building these resources, they create a lasting foundation for future generations. *However, today many families are facing crushing challenges having little family capital and these challenges are more acute in the Black family.*

The Existential Crisis of the Black Family

According to Dr. George C. Fraser, the Black community is facing an "existential crisis" stemming from the dramatic decline in marriage rates. He states: *"Of the five biggest challenges black people have for the next 100 years the number one challenge is the existential crisis of the black family."*

The current marriage rate within the Black community is cited as 34%, a significant drop from a historical rate of 85%.

- This decline is presented as a unique phenomenon, stating: *"This phenomenon of the existential crisis of our family only exists among African American black people. It does not exist on the continent or anywhere else in the world."* Noted is the disproportionate number of unmarried individuals with statistics such as: *"71 percent of our sisters are not married. 29 percent will never get married. 63 percent of*

24

our brothers are not married. 30 percent of them will never get married."

Correlation between Marriage Rates and Wealth:

Accordingly, he correlates declining marriage rates with lower household median income within the Black community. It highlights that the Black community has the lowest household median income ($55,000) and marriage rate (34%) compared to other ethnic groups.

The document presents a comparative analysis across different ethnic groups, listing East Indians ($104,000/year, 94% marriage rate), Chinese Asians ($110,000/year, 70% marriage rate), and Whites ($88,000/year, ~50% marriage rate), demonstrating a positive correlation between marriage rates and household income.

It specifically notes, "Household median income was dominated by white people. They were number one in this country. They no longer are number one. And there's a reason for it."

Projected Decline and Urgency:

- This suggests that the problem is getting worse and there is an urgency for it to be addressed: *"And projected based on facts and statistics, that if we do not fix this, because white folks say fixing this, our marriage rate will be in the low teens in the next 20 years. We must, this is an enormous challenge."*

The declining marriage rate and associated challenges are framed as requiring immediate action and a shift in focus within the community.

PART 2: Bringing All Together

My Personal Journey (Candid)

I come to this topic not just as an author or pastor or a husband and father. I approach this as one divinely call to the mission in 2020 to restore the family to divine order. As a young man I experienced a dysfunctional family. However, in 1985, my wife Valerie and I were wed. We have faced our own struggles over the years—balancing ministry and family life, raising children in a world that often opposes godly principles, and facing the challenges that come with being holdouts in a changing world while leading others. But through it all, we have leaned on the foundation of faith, prayer, and unity.

As I write this, I think of our Sunday evenings and holiday family gatherings, where laughter and conversation flow freely, and the sound of our grandchildren's voices fills the home.

Those moments remind me why God calls us to cherish and invest in our families. They are not just sources of personal joy but also instruments of His kingdom.

I must emphasize the importance of human flourishing and how to create it: *"The greatest malady, though financial wealth has its place is the loss of Spiritual Capital through poor parenting, absent fathers, shacking and unstable marriages. Human flourishing consist of growth in spiritual graces like virtue, love, faith, hope, resilience etc."*

Let us here agree that the breakdown of the family structure is hindering connectedness and the development of these important virtues and therefore human potential within the Black community at alarming rates.

Acknowledging this to be the greatest problem facing us today is the first step to bringing needed change. It is greater than the issues of racism, inequity, inequality, social justice, economic opportunity etc. Though it is the proverbial elephant in the room, politicians, sociologist as well as most preachers fail to give it the importance it is due. This is a huge problem because it is the family, the home that God designed to nurture truth, justice, health, education, respect for life, sexual purity and covenant living. Failure here is the number one problem in our culture. So, we must fix it."

The answer to this call is why I have dedicated myself and ministry to the establishment of **CFADD (**Christian Families Against Destructive Decisions). It was in 2020 that God gave me a mandate, for the purpose of influencing the building of strong families and strong family heritages by promoting a biblical worldview and a God first lifestyle. Thankfully today it has been embraced in seven states and by numerous individuals and pastors. You may learn more and become a Family Champion at CFADD at www.cfadd.org

Chapter 3: God's Design for Family

When I think about the purpose and power of family, my mind often returns to one of the most profound examples in the Bible: the story of Noah. His life and the unity of his family provide a vivid blueprint for how God intends families to function.

Noah's story is not just about survival during a catastrophic flood; it's about the power of obedience, faith, and collective effort within the family unit.

In Genesis 6, we find Noah living in a world consumed by sin and corruption. God, grieved by humanity's wickedness, decides to cleanse the earth through a flood. Yet, in this darkness, Noah finds favor in God's eyes. Why? Because Noah was a righteous man who walked faithfully with God and his family. (Genesis 6:9).

A Divine Calling

God's instructions to Noah were extraordinary: build an ark large enough to save his family and pairs of every animal species. This was no small task. The ark wasn't just a lifeboat; it was a testament to faith and obedience. But what stands out to me is that God didn't call Noah alone. He included Noah's family in His plan of redemption.

Imagine the conversations that must have taken place within Noah's household. The skepticism they must have faced from their neighbors. The sheer physical labor required to build an ark of such magnitude. Yet, through it all, Noah and his family remained unified. They worked together, prayed together, and trusted God together.

This is a powerful reminder that God's design for family extends beyond providing companionship and support. He intends for families to be instruments of His will, capable of accomplishing extraordinary things when united in faith.

The Role of Faith in Noah's Family

Faith and devotion was the cornerstone of Noah's family's success. Hebrews 11:7 tells us, *"By faith Noah, when warned about things not yet seen, in holy fear built an ark to save his family. By his faith he condemned the world and became heir of the righteousness that is in keeping with faith."*

Faith isn't just belief; it's action. Noah didn't just hear God's instructions and sit idly by. He acted, and his family followed his lead. This teaches us an important principle: faith starts with leadership.

As the head of his household, Noah's obedience set the tone for his family. But it wasn't a one-man show. His sons, Shem, Ham, and Japheth, alongside their wives, played essential roles in fulfilling God's plan. This unity exemplifies how families can achieve great things when they operate as a cohesive unit, rooted in faith.

Lessons from Noah's Ark

Noah's story provides several key lessons for modern families:

Leadership Requires Faithful Obedience

Noah's willingness to follow God's instructions, even when they seemed impossible, demonstrates the importance of trusting God's plan. As leaders within our homes—whether as parents, guardians, or mentors—we must lead by example, showing our families what it means to walk in faith.

Unity Multiplies Strength

Building the ark was not a task Noah could accomplish alone. His family's collaboration was essential. This reminds us that families are strongest when everyone contributes their unique strengths to a shared purpose.

God's Plan Includes Generations

God didn't just save Noah; He saved Noah's entire family. This highlights the importance of generational unity, and the role families play in passing down faith and values.

Obedience Brings Protection and Purpose

The ark wasn't just a means of survival; it was a vessel of God's grace and protection. When families align themselves with God's will, they find not only safety but also a sense of divine purpose.

A Personal Reflection

Noah's story resonates deeply with me because I've seen firsthand how faith and unity can carry a family through life's storms. I think back to moments in my own household when challenges threatened to overwhelm us. Whether it was financial uncertainty, the pressures of ministry, or the growing pains of raising children, the only way we overcame was by standing together in faith.

One particular moment stands out. Years ago, our church faced a significant trial that left our family in a season of uncertainty. It would have been easy for us to retreat into our own fears and frustrations. But instead, we came together as a family, much like Noah's household, and sought God's guidance. We prayed, fasted, and encouraged one another to trust that God was still in control.

Looking back, I see how that trial strengthened us, both as a family and as a ministry. It was a reminder that, just like Noah's family, we were never meant to face challenges alone. God equips families to support, encourage, and uplift one another so they can fulfill His purpose together.

God's Design for Your Family

The story of Noah is not just an ancient tale; it's a call to action for every family today. God's design hasn't changed. He still calls families to walk in faith, work together, and trust Him to guide their steps.

Whether your family is facing smooth waters or turbulent storms, the principles in Noah's story remain the same. Leadership grounded in faith, unity in purpose, and obedience to God's will can transform any household into a vessel of His grace.

As we continue this chapter, we'll explore how these principles apply to your family. We'll delve into practical ways to strengthen faith, build unity, and embrace God's design for your household. But for now, let Noah's story inspire you to see your family not just as a collection of individuals but as a powerful unit, called and equipped by God to do great things.

As we further analyze the narrative of Noah, we shall concentrate on the significant obedience that characterized his family's journey. Obedience is not a word that sits comfortably with many people today. In a world that values independence and self-determination, the idea of submitting to a higher authority often feels foreign, even restrictive. But Noah's story shows us that obedience to God is not a limitation; it is a pathway to freedom, purpose, and protection.

When God gave Noah the instructions for the ark, they were specific and detailed. The length, width, and height were exact. The materials—gopher wood—were specified. Even the number of decks and the type of food to be stored were outlined (Genesis 6:14-21). These details weren't suggestions; they were commands.

The Blessing of Obedience

Noah didn't argue with God. He didn't delay. He didn't cut corners to make the task easier. Instead, Genesis 6:22 tells us, *"Noah did everything just as God commanded him."*

This level of obedience must have required tremendous faith, not just from Noah but from his entire family. Imagine the years spent constructing the ark while the world around them continued as if nothing were wrong. Imagine the ridicule and doubt they must have endured from their neighbors. Yet Noah's obedience and his family's unity carried them through.

This is a powerful lesson for modern families. God's instructions, as laid out in His Word, may sometimes seem countercultural or even impractical. Principles like forgiveness, patience, humility, and sacrifice aren't always easy to apply in our daily lives. But when we choose obedience—both as individuals and as families—we align ourselves with God's will and open the door to His blessings.

Building the Ark: A Family Effort

The ark wasn't just Noah's project; it was a family endeavor. While Noah may have received the instructions directly from God, it's clear that his sons and their wives played crucial roles in bringing the vision to life.

This collaborative effort speaks to the importance of involving every family member in the pursuit of God's purposes. Too often, families operate in silos. Parents may pursue their faith individually while their children remain disconnected. Or one spouse might take on the spiritual leadership of the home while the other disengages.

Noah's story challenges us to break down these walls. Faith is not a solo journey; it is a collective one. Families that pray together, serve together, and worship together build stronger bonds and a deeper understanding of God's plan for their lives.

A Modern Parallel

I recall a family in our congregation who faced what seemed like an insurmountable challenge. Their oldest son, a teenager at the time, had fallen into the wrong crowd and begun making destructive decisions. The family felt helpless, unsure of how to guide him back.

Rather than giving up or pointing fingers, they came together in prayer and action. They sought God's guidance, unified in their commitment to help their son. The parents began incorporating family devotionals into their routine, even when their son refused to participate. The siblings wrote him notes of encouragement, reminding him of his worth and potential.

It wasn't an immediate transformation, but over time, the boy began to respond. Today, he is not only thriving but also leading a youth ministry of his own. This family's unity and obedience to God's principles made the impossible possible.

Lessons for Modern Families

The story of Noah and his family provides timeless principles that can transform our households today:

1. **Prioritize God's Instructions**

   Just as Noah followed God's specific instructions for building the ark, families must prioritize His Word in their decisions and actions. This means making time for scripture, prayer, and worship as foundational practices.

2. **Strengthen Unity Through Shared Goals**

   Noah's family worked together to fulfill God's command. Modern families can do the same by setting shared spiritual goals, such as serving in ministry, engaging in community outreach, or supporting one another's growth in faith.

3. **Embrace Faith During Uncertainty**

   Noah had never seen rain, let alone a flood, yet he trusted God's warning. Families today must learn to trust God's promises, even when the path ahead seems unclear.

4. **Lead with Obedience and Grace**

   Noah's leadership set the tone for his family's obedience. Whether you are a parent, spouse, or sibling, your example of faith and grace can inspire others to follow God's plan.

Noah's Covenant: A Legacy of Faith

The story of Noah doesn't end with the floodwaters receding. After the rain stopped, God made a covenant with Noah and his descendants, symbolized by a rainbow. In Genesis 9:12-13, God says, *"This is the sign of the covenant I am making between me and you and every living creature with you, a covenant for all generations to come: I have set my rainbow in the clouds, and it will be the sign of the covenant between me and the earth."*

This covenant wasn't just for Noah; it was for his family and the generations that followed. It's a reminder that our obedience and unity as families have a generational impact. The choices we make today don't just affect us; they shape the legacy we leave behind.

Our Existence is a Call to Action

As you reflect on Noah's story, consider the ark you are building within your own family. What are you constructing through your words, actions, and faith? Are you working together, or are there divisions that need healing?

God is calling your family to be a signal of His grace and a vessel of His purpose. Like Noah's family, you have the potential to make an eternal impact—not just within your household but in your community and beyond.

Let us move forward with this example, embracing God's design for family and committing to obedience, unity, and faith.

As we close our reflection on Noah's story, one more aspect stands out: the sheer magnitude of the ark's construction. This wasn't a small boat. It was a massive, multi-decked vessel capable of housing Noah's family, pairs of every kind of animal, and enough provisions to last through the flood. Scholars estimate it took decades to build—decades of labor, planning, and perseverance.

Now consider this: the ark was built in a time when rain was an unfamiliar concept, let alone a global flood. Noah and his family worked not with the confirmation of visible rain clouds but with the certainty of God's promise. This speaks volumes about the power of trust in God's word.

The Ark as a Symbol of Family Capital

The ark represents more than a physical structure; it symbolizes what families can achieve when they work together in faith and obedience. Every plank nailed into place, every joint sealed with pitch, was a testament to their unity. The ark became a shelter—not just from the floodwaters but also from doubt, fear, and the ridicule of the outside world.

In the same way, families today are called to build "arks" of their own. These aren't physical boats but spiritual and emotional sanctuaries where love, faith, and unity reign. These arks protect families from the storms of life: conflicts, financial struggles, societal pressures, and more. They are built through prayer, with purpose on purpose, and trust in God's plan.

The Bible is clear about the role of family in God's plan. From the very beginning, when God created Adam and Eve, He established the family as the cornerstone of His creation.

Genesis 1:28 says, "God blessed them and said to them, 'Be fruitful and increase in number; fill the earth and subdue it.'" Families were designed to reflect God's love and glory, serving as a training ground for faith and righteousness.

Consider the story of Noah. When God decided to save humanity from the flood, He didn't just use Noah; He used Noah's entire household. Noah's family's faith and obedience ensured that his family would play a pivotal role in God's plan. This is a powerful reminder that families, when united in faith, have the potential to accomplish extraordinary things.

The Untapped Potential in Modern Families

In today's world, many families face immense pressure. Busy schedules, generational divides, and the influence of technology often weaken the bonds that God intended to strengthen us. But it doesn't have to be this way. Families can rediscover their purpose and reclaim their power by returning to God's design.

This book is not just a call to action; it is a guide. Over the next chapters, we will explore what it means to cultivate love, strengthen faith, and build unity within the family. We will delve into the biblical principles that have shaped my own family and ministry and discuss practical strategies for strengthening your relationships.

My prayer is that as you read, you will see your family not as a source of frustration or a set of obligations but as a treasure trove of untapped potential. The same God who created the universe has placed you in your family for a reason. He has given you everything you need to thrive—not just for your own sake but for the sake of future generations.

Families are God's masterpiece, and when we align our homes with His principles, we unlock a power that can transform lives, communities, and even nations. Let us embark on this journey together, discovering the wealth that lies within and learning how to use it for God's glory.

When we talk about family capital, it's important to understand that this is not a concept reserved for extraordinary families or those who appear perfect from the outside. No family is without flaws. We all carry burdens, endure misunderstandings, and face challenges that test our resolve. But the beauty of God's design is that He doesn't require perfection. Instead, He calls us to commitment, faith, and love.

In my early years of ministry, I witnessed families transformed when they simply chose to embrace God's principles, no matter their circumstances. I recall one couple who came to me in a state of utter brokenness. They were on the verge of divorce, overwhelmed by financial strain, and burdened by years of unresolved conflict. As we talked, I realized they had been looking for solutions in all the wrong places—self-help books, advice from friends, even financial schemes. What they hadn't done was invite God into their family.

Through counseling and prayer, they began to rebuild, brick by brick, the foundation of their marriage. It wasn't an overnight transformation, but as they prioritized faith and communication, their home began to change. Today, they not only have a thriving marriage but have also become mentors to other couples in similar situations. This is the power of family capital. It starts small, often in the quiet moments of surrender to God, but its impact can be monumental.

Recognizing the Wealth Within

Many families fail to recognize the wealth they already possess. Society often teaches us to measure success in terms of material wealth—houses, cars, bank accounts—but God measures success differently. He looks at the love we share, the faith we cultivate, and the legacy we leave behind.

In Proverbs 22:6, we are reminded to "Train up a child in the way he should go; even when he is old, he will not depart from it." This verse speaks to the profound responsibility and privilege of shaping future generations. It's not about leaving behind money or possessions; it's about imparting values, wisdom, and faith. These are the treasures that cannot be taken away, no matter what challenges arise.

As a father, I've seen this firsthand. Raising five children wasn't always easy, especially while balancing the demands of ministry. There were nights when exhaustion made me want to retreat, and mornings when I questioned whether I was doing enough. But I held onto the truth that my role as a father was ordained by God. Every moment spent teaching, correcting, or simply listening was an investment—not just in my children's lives but in their future families as well.

The Role of Faith in Family Capital

Faith is the cornerstone of family capital. Without it, families are like ships without anchors, drifting wherever the tides of life take them. Faith provides direction, stability, and hope. It reminds us that even in our darkest moments, God is present, working all things for our good.

I think of the story of Joseph. Betrayed by his brothers and sold into slavery, Joseph had every reason to turn his back on his family. Yet, through his unwavering faith in God, he not only forgave them but also became the instrument of their salvation during a time of famine. His story teaches us that faith can heal even the deepest wounds and bring about reconciliation where there seemed to be none.

In my own family, faith has been our guiding light. Valerie and I have always made prayer a priority, not just as individuals but as a family. We have experienced test in countless ways over the years through ministry and family challenges however we had developed the family capital that was necessary to be victorious in each. One instance I remember a particular season when we faced a financial crisis after building our present church edifice that threatened to overwhelm us. Bills were piling up, and options were slim. But instead of panicking, we gathered our children and prayed. We asked God for provision, wisdom, and peace.

The answer didn't come immediately, but over time, doors began to open. Unexpected blessings arrived, and we were able to endure and overcome that storm with our faith intact. More importantly, our children witnessed firsthand the power of prayer and the faithfulness of God. Today, as they raise families of their own, they continue to rely on the principles we instilled in them during those tough times.

Laying the Foundation for What's Ahead

As we move forward in this journey together, I encourage you to take a moment to reflect on your own family. What are the strengths that God has already placed within your household? What areas need attention, healing, or growth?

This book is not about offering quick fixes or superficial solutions. It's about equipping you with the tools and understanding to cultivate the family God has called you to have. Whether you are a single parent, a newlywed couple, or a multigenerational household, the principles of family capital are universal. They transcend cultural, economic, and social boundaries because they are rooted in the unchanging Word of God.

I am not asking you to walk this path alone. Throughout these pages, I will share stories, biblical truths, and practical advice to help you recognize and unlock the untapped power within your family. My prayer is that by the time you finish this book, you will not only see your family differently but also approach your role within it with renewed purpose and passion.

The journey won't always be easy. It will require patience, humility, and faith. But I can promise you this: when you invest in your family, the returns are eternal.

As we delve deeper into the concept of family capital, it's essential to remember that this is not a fleeting idea but a God- ordained truth. The family was His design, established long before governments, organizations, or societies. Families are not just social units; they are divine constructs meant to reflect His love, nurture growth, and carry His message to the world.

I often tell those I counsel that if you want to see God's heart, look at the family. He chose to reveal Himself as a Father, demonstrating the kind of intimate and sacrificial love that forms the foundation of a thriving home. In fact, throughout scripture, God repeatedly uses familial language to describe His relationship with us. From referring to the church as His bride to calling believers His children, He underscores the sacredness of these bonds.

The Foundation of Family Capital: Love

The cornerstone of family capital is love—not the fleeting, conditional kind that fades with circumstances but the steadfast, enduring love that mirrors God's love for us. In 1 Corinthians 13:4-7, Paul writes: *"Love is patient, love is kind. It does not envy, it does not boast, it is not proud… It always protects, always trusts, always hopes, always perseveres."*

This kind of love is not always easy. It requires effort, humility, and sacrifice. As a young father, I had to learn this firsthand. There were days when my patience wore thin, and the demands of ministry seemed to leave little room for my family. But each time I felt overwhelmed, God reminded me of His love for me— unwavering, unconditional, and ever-present. It became clear that if I wanted my family to thrive, I needed to emulate that same love.

Love, however, is not just about emotions. It's about action. It's about creating an environment where every member feels valued, heard, and supported. Families flourish when love is not only expressed but lived out daily through service, forgiveness, and encouragement.

Forging Resilience Through Unity

Another key component of Family Capital is unity. A divided family cannot stand strong, nor can it withstand the storms of life. Jesus Himself said in **Mark 3:25**, *"If a house is divided against itself, that house cannot stand."* Families that are united, on the other hand, reflect the strength and power of God's design, becoming resilient in the face of challenges and unstoppable in achieving their God-given purpose.

Unity doesn't mean the absence of disagreements. In fact, healthy conflict can often lead to growth and deeper understanding. But unity does mean that, despite differences, a family remains committed to one another and their shared purpose in God. This kind of unity is a spiritual discipline, and Scripture is rich with principles that illustrate its importance and the blessings it brings.

Unity Strengthens Prayer and Releases Blessing

In **1 Peter 3:7**, husbands are instructed to live in unity with their wives so that their prayers will not be hindered. This underscores a critical truth: disunity can block spiritual power, while unity invites the presence and blessing of God into a family. Families that cultivate unity—praying together, supporting one another, and seeking God as a unit—unlock a spiritual strength that cannot be achieved in isolation.

The psalmist illustrates the anointing of unity in **Psalm 133:1– 2**: *"Behold, how good and how pleasant it is for brethren to dwell together in unity! It is like the precious oil upon the head, running down on the beard, the beard of Aaron, running down on the edge of his garments."*

Just as the oil flowed from Aaron's head to the hem of his robe, symbolizing the overflow of God's anointing, so too does the blessing of unity pour down upon a family, saturating each member with strength, peace, and divine favor.

Unity Unlocks the Power to Achieve Goals

Unity also has the power to amplify a family's ability to achieve their goals. In the story of the Tower of Babel, God Himself recognized the extraordinary potential of unity: *"Behold, the people are one, and they all have one language... now nothing that they propose to do will be withheld from them"* (Genesis 11:6).

Though the people's purpose in this story was misguided, the principle remains clear: when people are united in purpose, their capacity to accomplish great things is limitless. Imagine what a family could achieve when united in a God- honoring mission.

Whether it's overcoming financial hardship, ministering to their community, or raising children who walk in faith, families that work together in unity experience the fulfillment of *"nothing will be impossible"* (Matthew 17:20).

Over the years, I've seen countless examples of unity transforming families. One that stands out involves a family in our congregation who faced a life-altering challenge: a serious illness that left the mother bedridden. The weight of caring for her fell on her husband and children, and tensions began to rise as everyone struggled to adjust. But instead of allowing the stress to tear them apart, they chose to come together. They prayed as a family, divided responsibilities, and encouraged one another through every difficult moment.

Their journey wasn't easy, but their unity allowed them to face the challenge with strength and grace. Today, not only is the mother recovering, but the family is closer than ever. Their story is a testament to the power of unity in building resilience and overcoming adversity.

Faith: The Anchor in a Shifting World

In today's rapidly changing world, families often feel adrift. The pressures of modern life—financial instability, societal expectations, and the pervasive influence of technology—can erode the foundations of even the strongest households. But faith serves as an anchor, grounding families in something unchanging and eternal.

I've often shared with others how faith has been the unshakable foundation of my own family. From the early days of our marriage, Valerie and I faced the challenges of raising children in a culture that often opposes biblical values, it has been our shared faith in God that has sustained us and blessed us our family so richly.

Faith equips families with hope, even in the darkest times. It reminds us that we are not alone, that we serve a God who is not only present but also sovereign over every detail of our lives. When families come together to worship, pray, and seek God's guidance, they tap into a power far greater than their own.

A Call to Action

As you reflect on your family, I urge you to ask: What role does love play in your home? Are you united in purpose, or are there divisions that need healing? Is faith a cornerstone of your household, or has it been sidelined by the busyness of life?

These are not questions meant to bring guilt or condemnation but to inspire hope and action. The untapped power of your family is waiting to be discovered, and it starts with a willingness to surrender to God's design.

Throughout this book, we'll explore practical ways to cultivate love, build unity, and strengthen faith within your family. But remember, transformation doesn't happen overnight. It's a process, one that requires prayer, patience, and perseverance.

I promise you this: If you commit to investing in your family, the rewards will not only impact your household but also echo through generations to come. God has a plan for your family, one that is filled with purpose, joy, and blessings. It's time to unlock that plan and step into the abundant life He has prepared for you.

Every family has the potential to become a wellspring of strength, yet, potential alone is not enough. It must be recognized, nurtured, and activated. This begins with understanding the role God has given each family member and embracing the unique contributions they bring to the household.

As I reflect on the dynamics of my own family, I am reminded of how God equips us all differently yet calls us to unity. My wife, Valerie, has always been a source of wisdom and calm in our home. Her nurturing spirit has not only raised our five children but has also shaped countless lives in our church and community. In contrast, I often found myself in the role of the disciplinarian, the one who set boundaries and maintained order. Our different approaches were not a hindrance; they were complementary. Together, we built a home where love, respect, and faith flourished. Each of our children has been anointed with different gifts and talents that has enriched our lives and enabled our ministry.

This diversity within unity is no accident. God designed families to reflect His body, where every part has a purpose. In 1 Corinthians 12:12-14, Paul writes: *"For just as the body is one and has many members, and all the members of the body, though many, are one body, so it is with Christ."*

Likewise, families thrive when each member recognizes their role and contributes to the collective good.

Embracing the Unique Gifts of Each Member

One of the most important lessons I've learned is the value of recognizing and affirming the gifts God has placed within each family member. In our family, we've seen firsthand how God uses different strengths to achieve His purposes.

46

Our children, for example, each have distinct personalities and talents. One is an entrepreneur, full of ambition and creativity, while another is a compassionate caregiver who thrives in serving others. As parents, Valerie and I made it a priority to nurture their individual gifts while instilling shared values.

This doesn't mean the journey was without challenges. Like any family, we had moments of tension, disagreements, and growing pains. But through prayer and intentional effort, we learned to celebrate our differences and use them to strengthen our bond.

I encourage you to take time to identify the unique qualities within your family. What strengths does each person bring to the table? How can those strengths be used to glorify God and serve others? When families operate in their God-given roles, they become unstoppable forces for good.

The Ripple Effect of Strong Families

Strong families don't just benefit their own members; they create a ripple effect that impacts their communities, churches, and even future generations. I've witnessed this time and again in my ministry. Families that prioritize love, faith, and unity inspire others to do the same. They become pillars of their neighborhoods, sources of encouragement for friends, and examples for their children's peers.

Consider the story of Abraham in Genesis. God's covenant with Abraham wasn't just about him; it was about the generations that would follow. In Genesis 17:7, God says, *"I will establish my covenant between me and you and your offspring after you throughout their generations for an everlasting covenant."*

This promise reminds us that the decisions we make today have eternal significance. By investing in our families, we contribute to a legacy that extends far beyond our lifetimes.

I often think about the organization I founded, Christian Families Against Destructive Decisions (CFADD). Its mission is to promote a biblical worldview and encourage families to build strong heritages rooted in God's principles. Through CFADD, I've seen families transformed as they commit to prioritizing their faith and making intentional choices that align with God's will.

These families remind me of what's possible when we unlock the untapped power of family capital. They face challenges like everyone else, but their faith gives them the strength to overcome. They aren't perfect, but they are purposeful. And their impact reaches far beyond their immediate circles.

Practical Steps to Begin the Journey

If you're wondering where to start, let me offer a few simple steps to begin activating the family capital within your household:

1. **Pray Together**
   Make prayer a daily practice. Whether it's a quick prayer before meals or a longer family devotional time, inviting God into your home sets the tone for unity and purpose.

2. **Cultivate Open Communication**
   Create an environment where everyone feels heard. Encourage each family member to share their thoughts, dreams, and concerns. This builds trust and strengthens relationships.

3. **Set a Family Mission**
What does your family stand for? Take time to define your shared values and goals. Write them down and revisit them regularly to stay aligned.

4. **Serve Together**
Find ways to serve others as a family. Volunteer at your church, help a neighbor, or participate in community outreach. Serving together strengthens a sense of purpose and connection.

These are small but powerful steps that can lead to lasting change. Remember, transformation doesn't happen overnight, but every step of faith brings you closer to God's design for your family.

A Vision for What's Ahead

As we close this chapter, I want to leave you with a vision of what's possible. Imagine a home filled with love and laughter, where faith is the foundation, and every member feels valued. Imagine a family that not only supports one another but also serves as a light to those around them.

This is the power of family capital. It's not about perfection; it's about progress. It's about choosing every day to walk in God's will and trusting Him to do the rest. Let's continue this journey together, one step at a time, as we explore how to unlock the untapped potential within our families.

As we close the foundation of this book, I want to reflect on the broader implications of family capital. It's easy to see families as isolated units, self-contained in their struggles and triumphs. However, the truth is that families are the backbone of communities, the bedrock of churches, and the building blocks of society. When families thrive, so does everything around them.

God designed families to function as His vessels of love and influence. A strong family isn't just a blessing to its members; it's a blessing to the world. Families with shared faith and purpose have the power to affect change on a scale far greater than they often realize.

The Larger Mission of Families

Think of families as small, self-sustaining ministries. Each one has a calling, a mission, and a divine mandate. Some families are called to lead, others to serve, and others still to nurture. Regardless of the specific role, every family has a purpose in God's kingdom.

I am reminded of Joshua's declaration in Joshua 24:15: *"But as for me and my household, we will serve the Lord."* This wasn't just a statement of personal conviction; it was a family mission. Joshua understood that his family was a unit, designed to fulfill God's purposes together.

Today, that same call applies to every household. Whether you are a family of two or a family of twenty, God has a plan for you. But to step into that plan, families must first align themselves with His will.

Overcoming Barriers to Family Capital

As I've mentioned before, modern families face unique challenges that can obstruct the flow of family capital. From cultural influences on generational divides, these barriers can make it difficult to live out the biblical vision of family.

One of the most common barriers is a lack of time. In our fast-paced world, families often find themselves pulled in a hundred different directions. Work, school, extracurricular activities, and technology all compete for attention, leaving little room for meaningful connection. But the truth is, families don't grow stronger by accident. It takes intentional effort to create space for prayer, conversation, and togetherness. I encourage you to think of your family as a garden. If you neglect it, weeds will overtake it. But if you tend to it—watering it with love, fertilizing it with faith, and pruning it with care—it will flourish.

The Role of Leadership in the Family

Another key factor in unlocking family capital is leadership. Every family needs a leader, someone who sets the tone, casts the vision, and ensures that the household remains aligned with God's purposes.

For me, that role has often been a humbling one. As the spiritual leader of my home, I've had to make difficult decisions, admit my mistakes, and remain steadfast in prayer. Leadership isn't about being perfect; it's about being present and purposeful.

Ephesians 5:23 reminds us, *"For the husband is the head of the wife as Christ is the head of the church, his body, of which he is the Savior."* This doesn't mean dictatorship; it means servanthood. Just as Christ leads the church with love, sacrifice, and grace, so must the leaders of families guide their households.

For single-parent families or households where roles differ, the principle remains the same: leadership is about seeking God's will and guiding the family with wisdom and love.

A Call to See the Family as God Sees It

As we end this chapter, I want to challenge you to see your family through God's eyes. He doesn't see brokenness, shortcomings, or failures. He sees potential, purpose, and power. Every family, no matter its current state, can become a source of light and strength. It starts with a willingness to surrender to God's plan and a commitment to take small but intentional steps toward growth.

What would happen if every family embraced this calling? What if every household became a place where love, faith, and unity reigned supreme? Imagine the impact on our churches, communities, and the world at large.

Looking Ahead

The journey we've begun in this chapter is just the beginning. In the chapters to come, we'll explore practical ways to build love, cultivate faith, and create a legacy of unity within your family. We'll draw from scripture, personal stories, and real-life examples to guide you every step of the way.

It is my prayer that this book will inspire you, challenge you, and equip you to unlock the untapped power within your family. Together, we will rediscover the divine potential of family capital and learn how to use it to glorify God in every aspect of our lives.

Let us take the next step with hearts open to His will and a determination to walk in His ways. Your family's best days are ahead, and it begins now.

Building Your Family's Ark

Every family has the capacity to build an ark of faith, but it requires effort and vision. Here are some practical ways to begin:

1. **Establish a Spiritual Foundation**

   Just as Noah built his ark according to God's blueprint; families must build their lives on God's Word. This means prioritizing scripture, prayer, and worship as non- negotiable parts of daily life.

   Start small, perhaps with a weekly family devotional or a shared Bible reading. Make church attendance a family commitment, not an optional activity.

2. **Strengthen Relationships Within the Family**

   Noah's family had to work together to build the ark. Similarly, modern families must prioritize communication, teamwork, and mutual respect.

   Set aside time for family meetings where everyone can share their thoughts and concerns.

   Create opportunities for collaboration, whether through household projects, family outings, or shared responsibilities.

3. **Prepare for Storms Before They Come**

   The ark was built before the floodwaters arrived. In the same way, families must prepare for challenges before they arise by cultivating resilience and faith.

   Teach children biblical principles so they are equipped to face the world's challenges.

Strengthen a culture of forgiveness and grace, recognizing that no family is without mistakes or conflicts.

Facing Ridicule with Faith

One of the most striking aspects of Noah's story is the ridicule he likely endured. Imagine the skepticism and mockery from those who didn't believe a flood was coming. Yet Noah didn't let the opinions of others deter him. He remained steadfast in his calling, knowing that his obedience was ultimately to God, not man.

Families today face similar pressures. The world often dismisses or ridicules biblical values, labeling them as outdated or irrelevant. But just as Noah's faith proved to be his strength, so too can modern families find courage in God's promises.

I've seen this firsthand in my work with Christian Families Against Destructive Decisions (CFADD). Families who choose to live by a God-first lifestyle often face criticism, especially when they prioritize spiritual practices over societal norms. Yet these families also experience profound blessings—peace, unity, and a legacy that endures.

The Legacy of Noah's Family

Noah's story didn't end when the ark came to rest on Mount Ararat. His family emerged into a renewed world, tasked with rebuilding humanity. This underscores a critical truth: families aren't just about survival; they are about renewal and legacy.

After the flood, God blessed Noah and his sons, saying, *"Be fruitful and increase in number; fill the earth"* (Genesis 9:1).

This blessing wasn't just for Noah—it was for his descendants, a promise that their faith and obedience would bear fruit for generations.

Your family has the same potential. The choices you make today—the prayers you pray, the principles you uphold, the love you cultivate—are seeds that will bear fruit for years to come.

A Personal Challenge

I want to challenge you to think about the ark you are building within your family. What kind of structure are you creating?

Are you building on the solid foundation of God's Word, or are you relying on shaky materials like worldly success, convenience, or personal pride?

It's never too late to start anew. Just as Noah built his ark plank by plank, families can rebuild their foundations one step at a time.

Begin by identifying one area where your family can grow— whether it's in faith, communication, or unity.

Set small, achievable goals, and celebrate progress along the way.

Looking Forward

Noah's story is a powerful reminder that families are at the heart of God's plan. As we move into the next chapter, we will explore the role of love in building strong family bonds. Love is the glue that holds families together, the fuel that powers their efforts, and the light that guides them through darkness.

But for now, let Noah's example inspire you to embrace your family's potential. Just as his obedience and unity saved his household, so too can your faith and love transform your family into a beacon of God's grace.

As we draw closer to the heart of Noah's story, it's crucial to understand the profound impact obedience and unity within a family can have, not just on their immediate survival but also on their long-term legacy. The story of Noah reminds us that God works through families to achieve His purposes. He doesn't call us to perfection but to faithfulness, trust, and action.

The Ripple Effect of Family Faith

Noah's obedience didn't just save his immediate family; it became the foundation for humanity's renewal. His actions demonstrated the far-reaching power of faith and unity within a household. This principle applies to families today. When we align ourselves with God's will and work together in faith, our impact extends far beyond our home.

I've seen this ripple effect in my own family and ministry. One example that comes to mind involves a young couple who joined our church during a particularly tumultuous season in their lives. They had been struggling with marital discord, financial instability, and feelings of hopelessness.

Through counseling and prayer, they began to rebuild their foundation—not on worldly advice but on God's Word. They started small: daily prayers, attending church as a family, and setting aside time to talk openly about their struggles. Over time, their transformation was evident. Not only did their relationship strengthen, but they also became leaders in our congregation, mentoring other couples facing similar challenges.

This is the ripple effect of family faith. When one household chooses to live in obedience to God, it inspires others to do the same, creating a chain reaction of hope and renewal.

Family Roles in God's Plan

Noah's family illustrates the importance of each member playing their role in God's plan. While Noah received the vision and instructions, his sons and their wives contributed to the execution of the plan. They worked together, each bringing their unique skills and strengths to the task.

In today's families, the concept of shared roles is just as vital. Parents, children, and even extended family members all have unique contributions to make.

- **Parents as Spiritual Leaders**
    - Parents are called to be the spiritual anchors of their homes, modeling faith and teaching God's principles to their children. Ephesians 6:4 instructs, *"Fathers, do not provoke your children to anger, but bring them up in the discipline and instruction of the Lord."*

This doesn't mean parents must have all the answers, but they must prioritize spiritual growth in their homes, creating an environment where God's presence is central.

- **Children as Participants in Faith**
    - Children, too, play a role in building family unity. As they grow, they can contribute through acts of service, shared prayer, and openness to learning biblical truths. Proverbs 1:8-9 says, *"Listen, my son, to your father's instruction and do not forsake your mother's*

teaching. They are a garland to grace your head and a chain to adorn your neck."

Encouraging children to take ownership of their faith early sets the stage for lifelong spiritual growth.

- **Extended Family as Support Systems**
  - In many cultures, extended family members—grandparents, aunts, uncles—play an integral role in passing down values and providing support. Noah's family, though small in number, showed us the power of multigenerational unity in achieving God's purposes.

The Cost of Obedience

Obedience often comes with a cost. For Noah and his family, it meant years of labor, enduring ridicule, and stepping into an unknown future. They had to trust God completely, even when His instructions didn't make sense to the world around them.

Modern families face similar challenges. Choosing to live by biblical principles may invite criticism or even alienation from a culture that often prioritizes self-interest over faith and community. But as Noah's story shows us, the rewards of obedience far outweigh the sacrifices.

When families remain steadfast in their faith, they create a legacy that endures. They may not see the full impact of their obedience in their lifetime, but future generations will reap the benefits of their faithfulness.

Leaving a God-Centered Legacy

Noah's story didn't end with the flood. It continued through his descendants, who carried forward the faith and obedience that saved them. This is a reminder that families are not just about the present; they are about the future.

Every choice you make as a family—every prayer, every act of kindness, every moment spent teaching your children about God—plants seeds that will grow into a legacy.

- **Focus on Values That Last**
  Material wealth can be lost, but the spiritual wealth of love, faith, and unity endures. Proverbs 13:22 says, *"A good man leaves an inheritance to his children's children."* The inheritance spoken of here is far greater than money; it is the inheritance of a life lived in faith.

- **Celebrate Milestones of Faith**
  Just as Noah's family celebrated God's covenant after the flood, modern families can mark significant moments in their spiritual journey. Whether it's a baptism, a family prayer answered, or a child's first act of service, these milestones strengthen faith and unity.

A Personal Reflection

When I think of legacy, I often reflect on my role as a husband, father, and grandfather. Each day, I ask myself: What am I leaving behind for my children and grandchildren? Am I teaching them to trust God, to love one another, and to serve their community? It's a humbling thought, but it's also a motivating one. Legacy isn't built in a day; it's built over a lifetime of small, faithful choices.

Looking Ahead

As we conclude this chapter, let the story of Noah inspire you to see your family through the lens of God's design. Every family has the potential to be a vessel of His grace, a source of strength, and a light to the world.

In the next chapter, we will explore the foundational role of love in building strong, united families. Love is the heartbeat of every household, the glue that binds us together, and the reflection of God's character in our lives.

But for now, let us commit to building our own "arks" of faith and unity, trusting that God's plans for our families are far greater than we can imagine.

As we bring this chapter to a close, it's important to reflect on the overarching theme of Noah's story: God's design for family is rooted in faith, unity, and purpose. Families are not passive entities; they are active participants in God's redemptive plan. When we embrace this role, we unlock the potential within our households to glorify God and impact the world around us.

A Family's Responsibility to the World

Noah's family wasn't just saved for their sake. Their survival carried with it the responsibility of rebuilding humanity. This same principle applies to us today. Families are called not just to exist but to contribute—to their communities, their churches, and the generations that follow.

In Matthew 5:14-16, Jesus says, *"You are the light of the world. A town built on a hill cannot be hidden. Neither do people light a lamp and put it under a bowl. Instead they put it on its stand, and it gives light to everyone in the house. In the same way, let your light shine before others, that they may see your good deeds and glorify your Father in heaven."*

This passage reminds us that families have the power to illuminate the world with God's love and grace. When families operate in unity and obedience, they become living examples of His goodness, inspiring others to seek Him.

The Power of Multigenerational Devotion to God

Noah's family wasn't perfect, but they were faithful. After the flood, his sons went on to populate the earth, carrying forward the legacy of obedience and trust in God. This shows us the importance of multigenerational faith—passing down biblical principles, stories of God's faithfulness, and the commitment to follow His will.

In my own family, I've seen how this principle plays out. When my wife Valerie and I first began raising our children, we made a deliberate decision to center our household on God's Word. This meant not just attending church but making faith a daily practice.

We prayed together, studied the Bible together, and made decisions as a family based on what we believed God was calling us to do. Now, as I watch my grandchildren and great- grandchildren grow, I see the fruits of those efforts. They are carrying forward the values we instilled, creating their own legacies of faith.

This isn't unique to our family. Every household has the capacity to cultivate multigenerational faith. It starts with intentionality and a commitment to make God the center of your home.

Steps to Strengthen Multigenerational Faith

1. **Share Your Testimony**
   Every family has a story of God's faithfulness. Share it with your children and grandchildren so they can see how God has worked in your life.

   Talk about how God provided during difficult times.

   Share specific examples of answered prayers or moments when His guidance was clear.

2. **Encourage Participation in Faith Practices**
   Make devotion to God a family affair. Invite younger generations to participate in prayer, worship, and acts of service.

   Create opportunities for children to lead prayers or read scripture during family devotionals.

   Celebrate spiritual milestones, such as baptisms, with family-wide recognition and support.

3. **Model a God-First Lifestyle**
   Children and grandchildren learn by watching. Model integrity, generosity, and faithfulness in your daily life.

   Show them how to handle challenges with grace and prayer.

   Demonstrate the joy that comes from serving God and others.

The Role of the Church in Supporting Families

While the family is the primary institution for spiritual growth, the church plays a vital role in supporting and equipping families. Just as Noah's family relied on God's instructions to guide them, modern families can lean on the church for encouragement, resources, and community.

Your churches should provide:

- **Teaching**: Sermons and Bible studies that address family dynamics and spiritual growth.

- **Mentorship**: Opportunities for older couples or individuals to mentor younger families.

- **Fellowship**: Events and programs that strengthen relationships among families, creating a support network.

As a pastor, I have seen the incredible impact a strong church community can have on families. When families feel supported and connected, they are better equipped to overcome life's challenges and fulfill God's purpose.

Looking Ahead: The Power of Love

As we transition to the next chapter, we'll focus on the central role of love in God's design for families. Love is the foundation of every healthy relationship, the driving force behind unity, and the clearest reflection of God's character within the home.

But for now, take a moment to reflect on what we've learned from Noah's story. What steps can you take today to strengthen your family's faith, unity, and purpose? Whether it's starting a new family tradition, sharing your testimony, or committing to daily prayer, every action brings you closer to God's vision for your household.

Your family is not just a collection of individuals. It is a divine institution, called and equipped to make a difference. Together, let us build our "arks" of faith, trusting that God will guide us through every storm and into His promises.

Chapter 4: Love an Emotional Wealth in Families

Love is the cornerstone of every strong family. It is the thread that weaves through every relationship, every challenge, and every triumph. Without love, a family cannot thrive. Yet, in today's fast-paced world, love is often overshadowed by busyness, conflict, and distractions. We assume it will always be there, quietly holding everything together. However, love requires more than assumption—it demands intention, effort, and action.

In 1 Corinthians 13:4-7, Paul paints a vivid picture of love: *"Love is patient, love is kind. It does not envy, it does not boast, it is not proud. It does not dishonor others, it is not self-seeking, it is not easily angered, it keeps no record of wrongs. Love does not delight in evil but rejoices with the truth. It always protects, always trusts, always hopes, always perseveres."*

This passage is often read at weddings, but its relevance extends far beyond romantic relationships. It is a blueprint for how families can cultivate emotional wealth through love.

Love, according to Paul, is not just a feeling—it is a set of actions and attitudes that reflect the character of Christ.

The Transformative Power of Love

In my role as a pastor of 49 years, I have seen countless instances of how love transforms families. I recall a young man who came to me burdened by anger and resentment toward his father. Their relationship had been strained for years due to misunderstandings and unmet expectations. The young man was ready to give up on any hope of reconciliation, convinced that the damage was irreversible.

But then he did something remarkable. He chose to love indeed. Not the easy, superficial kind of love, but the kind that required humility, forgiveness, and patience. He began reaching out to his father—not with accusations or demands but with kindness and grace. Over time, their relationship began to heal. The walls of bitterness crumbled, and in their place grew a bond rooted in mutual respect and understanding.

This is the power of love. It breaks down barriers, heals wounds, and creates an environment where growth and unity can flourish.

Creating a Culture of Love in Your Home

Love doesn't happen by accident. It must be cultivated, nurtured, and prioritized. Here are some practical ways to create a culture of love within your family:

1. **Express Love Daily**

   Love is most powerful when it is expressed regularly. This can be as simple as saying, "I love you," offering a hug, or showing appreciation for something a family member has done.

   Words of affirmation, such as, "I'm proud of you," or, "I appreciate all you do," go a long way in making family members feel valued.

   Small acts of service, like cooking a favorite meal or helping with chores, demonstrate love in action.

2. **Practice Active Listening**

   One of the greatest ways to show love is by giving your full attention. When a family member speaks, listen without interrupting, judging, or offering solutions. Sometimes, the greatest gift you can give is simply being present.

3. **Forgive Freely**

   Every family experiences conflict, but love requires us to let go of grudges and extend forgiveness. Ephesians 4:32 reminds us, *"Be kind to one another, tenderhearted, forgiving one another, as God in Christ forgave you."*

   Forgiveness doesn't mean forgetting or excusing harmful behavior; it means releasing the burden of resentment and choosing to move forward in love.

4. **Celebrate Each Other**

   Families thrive when members feel seen and appreciated. Take time to celebrate achievements, both big and small, and acknowledge the unique gifts and contributions of each person.

   Create traditions that honor individual milestones, such as birthdays or personal achievements.

Love as a Reflection of God's Character

At its core, love reflects God's character. In 1 John 4:16, we are reminded, *"God is love. Whoever lives in love lives in God, and God in them."* When we love one another, we mirror God's love for us, creating a home environment that radiates His presence.

As a father, I have often found myself overwhelmed by the depth of God's love. It is patient when I am impatient. It is kind when I am harsh. It forgives when I fall short. This realization humbles me and reminds me of my responsibility to model that same love to my family.

One of the most profound ways to teach love is by living it. Children learn more from what they see than what they hear. When they witness parents treating each other with respect, resolving conflicts with grace, and prioritizing one another's needs, they internalize those values and carry them forward into their own relationships.

A Personal Reflection

When I think about the role of love in my family, I am reminded of the early years of my marriage to Valerie. Like any young couple, we had our share of disagreements and adjustments. There were moments when pride threatened to drive a wedge between us. But each time, love brought us back.

We learned that love isn't about being right; it's about being kind. It's about putting the other person's needs above your own and choosing grace over frustration. Those lessons became the foundation of our relationship, and they have guided us through nearly four decades of marriage.

Looking Ahead

As we continue this chapter, we will explore how love builds resilience, strengthens forgiveness, and creates a legacy of emotional wealth within families. Love isn't just a feeling; it's the engine that drives a healthy, thriving household.

For now, I encourage you to reflect on the role of love in your family. How is it expressed? Where is it lacking? And what steps can you take today to strengthen it?

Although love binds families together its power extends far beyond maintaining relationships. Love strengthens resilience, strengthens healing, and creates a foundation upon which families can weather life's storms. When love is prioritized and practiced, it becomes a source of emotional wealth—a kind of richness that no financial prosperity or worldly success can replace.

Love as the Foundation of Resilience

Families that are grounded in love are better equipped to face adversity. Love provides a sense of security and belonging that fortifies individuals against the trials of life. Consider the words of Ecclesiastes 4:12: *"Though one may be overpowered, two can defend themselves. A cord of three strands is not quickly broken."* Love is that third strand, strengthening the bond between family members and creating unity that withstands external pressures.

I recall a family in our church who faced what seemed like an insurmountable crisis. The father had lost his job, and the financial strain threatened to unravel their household. But instead of allowing fear and frustration to divide them, they chose to support one another in love. The mother encouraged her husband daily, reminding him of his worth and potential. The children offered to help with chores and expenses, contributing what they could to lighten the load.

Over time, their situation improved, but what stood out most was the strength of their bond. They emerged from the crisis not just intact but closer than ever. This is the power of love: it doesn't eliminate challenges, but it gives families the resilience to overcome them together.

Healing Through Love

Love is also the key to healing—both within families and in individual hearts. In my years of ministry, I've counseled countless families fractured by conflict, misunderstanding, or neglect. Time and again, I've witnessed how love, expressed through patience and forgiveness, can mend even the deepest wounds.

Forgiveness is a particularly powerful expression of love. It is not a sign of weakness but of strength, requiring humility and grace. Colossians 3:13 reminds us, *"Bear with each other and forgive one another if any of you has a grievance against someone. Forgive as the Lord forgave you."*

One story that has stayed with me involves two siblings who had been estranged for years due to a misunderstanding over their late parents' estate. The bitterness had festered to the point where they refused to speak to one another. After years of separation, one of them decided to extend an olive branch. He reached out, not to demand an apology or settle old scores, but simply to say, "I miss you, and I love you."

That simple act of vulnerability was the first step toward reconciliation. It didn't erase the hurt overnight, but it opened the door to healing. Today, their relationship is stronger than ever, a testament to the transformative power of love.

Practical Ways to Strengthen Healing Love

If your family is carrying wounds—whether from past conflicts, unmet expectations, or unresolved pain—here are some practical ways to begin cultivating healing through love:

1. **Start with Prayer**
   Healing begins with inviting God into the situation. Pray for wisdom, patience, and the strength to love even when it's difficult.

2. **Acknowledge the Hurt**
   Ignoring pain doesn't make it go away. Take time to acknowledge what has happened, allowing each person to express their feelings without judgment.

3. **Take the First Step**
   Be the one to extend an olive branch, even if you feel the other person is at fault. Love doesn't wait for perfect conditions; it acts in faith.

4. **Focus on Rebuilding Trust**
   Healing takes time. Be consistent in your words and actions, showing through your behavior that you are committed to rebuilding the relationship.

Love as a Legacy

One of the most profound aspects of love is its generational impact. The love you cultivate within your family today sets the tone for future generations. Children who grow up in a home filled with love are more likely to carry those values into their own relationships, creating a ripple effect of emotional wealth.

Proverbs 22:6 says, *"Train up a child in the way he should go; even when he is old he will not depart from it."* Teaching children how to love—through example, encouragement, and discipline—lays a foundation for healthy, God-centered relationships that extend far beyond your home.

In my own family, I've seen this play out across generations. Valerie and I worked hard to create an environment where love was not just felt but expressed openly. We encouraged our children to share their feelings, support one another, and resolve conflicts with grace.

Now, as I watch my grandchildren interact, I see the fruits of those efforts. The kindness, patience, and respect they show one another reflect the love that has been passed down.

A Challenge for Your Family

As you reflect on the role of love in your family, I want to challenge you to take one intentional step toward building or strengthening that love. It could be as simple as writing a heartfelt note to a family member, setting aside time for a one- on-one conversation, or initiating a family prayer time.

Love is not passive; it is active and intentional. It requires effort, but the rewards are eternal. As Paul reminds us in 1 Corinthians 13:8, *"Love never fails."*

Looking Ahead

In the next part of this chapter, we'll explore how love, combined with faith and unity, creates a powerful force for transformation. Love is not just an emotion; it is a calling, a reflection of God's character, and the most valuable inheritance we can leave for future generations.

For now, let love guide your thoughts, words, and actions. Your family is a gift from God, and love is the key to unlocking its full potential.

Love as a Reflection of God's Nature

Love is not merely an emotion; it is the essence of who God is. In 1 John 4:16 (KJV), we read, *"And we have known and believed the love that God hath to us. God is love; and he that dwelleth in love dwelleth in God, and God in him."* When families prioritize love, they reflect God's nature and invite His presence into their homes.

This truth is especially profound when we consider how God demonstrates His love for us. Romans 5:8 (KJV) tells us, *"But God commended his love toward us, in that, while we were yet sinners, Christ died for us."* If God's love is sacrificial and unconditional, so too must our love within the family be selfless and enduring.

I often encourage families to view love not as something they give only when it's convenient, but as a commitment. Love shows up in the moments when patience is tested, when forgiveness feels undeserved, and when sacrifice is required. This is the kind of love that transforms households.

Building Unity Through Love

Unity is one of the greatest fruits of love. A family united by love can overcome challenges that might otherwise divide them. Psalm 133:1 (KJV) beautifully states, *"Behold, how good and how pleasant it is for brethren to dwell together in unity!"*

Unity doesn't mean there will never be disagreements. Every family experiences conflict, but love provides the tools to navigate those moments with grace. Here are some practical ways to use love as a foundation for unity:

1. **Prioritize Relationships Over Being Right**
   - Arguments often escalate because someone feels the need to win. Instead, focus on preserving the relationship. Proverbs 15:1 (KJV) reminds us, *"A soft answer turneth away wrath: but grievous words stir up anger."*

2. **Seek to Understand Before Being Understood**
   - When conflicts arise, take time to listen to the other person's perspective. This act of love

demonstrates respect and opens the door for resolution.

3. **Pray Together**
   - Prayer is one of the most unifying practices a family can engage in. When you pray together, you invite God's peace into your home and strengthen your bond as a family. Matthew 18:20 (KJV) assures us, *"For where two or three are gathered together in my name, there am I in the midst of them."*

Love and Forgiveness: Two Sides of the Same Coin

Love and forgiveness are inseparable. To love deeply means to forgive often, just as Christ forgives us. Ephesians 4:32 (KJV) exhorts us, *"And be ye kind one to another, tenderhearted, forgiving one another, even as God for Christ's sake hath forgiven you."*

I once counseled a father and son whose relationship had been strained for years. The father struggled to let go of his disappointment over choices his son had made, while the son harbored resentment for feeling misunderstood. Their breakthrough came when both realized they were holding onto the past rather than extending forgiveness. They began to see each other through the lens of love, focusing on reconciliation instead of blame.

Forgiveness doesn't erase the past, but it removes its power to control the future. In the same way, love doesn't ignore mistakes; it creates a pathway for healing and growth.

Teaching Love to the Next Generation

As parents and guardians, one of the most important legacies we can leave is the example of love. Children learn how to love by observing their parents. They internalize not only how love is expressed but also how conflicts are resolved and forgiveness is offered.

Proverbs 22:6 (KJV) advises, *"Train up a child in the way he should go: and when he is old, he will not depart from it."* Training children in love means showing them how to treat others with kindness, patience, and respect. It means modeling humility and showing them that love sometimes requires putting others' needs before your own.

One practice my wife Valerie and I adopted early in our marriage was speaking blessings over our children. We would pray for them daily, asking God to fill their hearts with love and compassion. As they grew, we encouraged them to do the same for one another, cultivating a spirit of love that extended beyond our home.

A Prayer for Your Family

As you reflect on the role of love in your household, I encourage you to take a moment to pray for your family. Here is a prayer you might use as a starting point:

Heavenly Father, thank You for the gift of family and the love You have shown us through Christ. Help us to reflect Your love in our home, to forgive as You forgive, and to build unity through patience and kindness. May our family be a testimony of Your grace and a light to the world. In Jesus' name, Amen.

Looking Ahead

In the next part of this chapter, we'll explore how love not only strengthens individual families but also has the power to transform communities. Love is not just a private act; it is a ripple effect that spreads wherever it is sown.

For now, let us strive to love deeply, forgive freely, and reflect the character of God in every interaction within our families.

Love within the family is not just a personal blessing; it is a force that has the power to transform communities and societies. When families are rooted in love, they become beacons of light, extending the grace and kindness they experience at home to the world around them. This ripple effect of love reflects God's design for humanity.

The Ripple Effect of Love

When love flows freely within a family, it naturally extends outward. In John 13:35 (KJV), Jesus says, *"By this shall all men know that ye are my disciples, if ye have love one to another."* The love we demonstrate within our families serves as a testimony to others, showing them the character of God.

Strong, loving families contribute to healthier communities. Children raised in homes where love is modeled learn to treat others with kindness and respect. Parents who extend love to their neighbors and community members create a culture of compassion and service. This ripple effect has the potential to transform schools, workplaces, churches, and beyond.

I've seen this principle at work through Christian Families Against Destructive Decisions (CFADD). Families who commit to living out biblical principles often inspire others to do the same. Their love becomes a catalyst for change, encouraging other families to prioritize faith, unity, and service.

Love in Action: Serving Others as a Family

One of the most powerful ways to extend love beyond the home is through acts of service. Families that serve together not only strengthen their own bonds but also reflect God's love to the world. Galatians 5:13 (KJV) reminds us, *"For, brethren, ye have been called unto liberty; only use not liberty for an occasion to the flesh, but by love serve one another."*

Here are some practical ways your family can put love into action:

1. **Volunteer Together**

   Whether it's serving at a food bank, visiting the elderly, or participating in a community clean-up, volunteering as a family strengthens unity and demonstrates love in action.

2. **Support a Neighbor in Need**

   Look for opportunities to assist those in your immediate community. It could be helping a neighbor with yard work, providing a meal for someone recovering from illness, or offering transportation to those who need it.

3. **Engage in Church Ministry**

   Get involved in your local church as a family. Serve in areas like children's ministry, hospitality, or outreach programs. This not only strengthens your church community but also reinforces the importance of service in your children's lives.

The Transformative Power of Love in Communities

When families take their love beyond their homes, they become agents of change. Love has the power to heal divisions, strengthen understanding, and build bridges where there were once walls. Proverbs 10:12 (KJV) states, *"Hatred stirreth up strifes: but love covereth all sins."*

I once counseled a family who had been deeply involved in their community. They regularly hosted gatherings, offered support to struggling neighbors, and participated in local outreach efforts. When a conflict arose within their neighborhood, they were instrumental in resolving it—not by taking sides, but by bringing people together in love and understanding.

Their actions reminded me that love is not passive; it is active, intentional, and often requires stepping into difficult situations. Yet the rewards are profound. Through their efforts, this family not only restored peace in their community but also inspired others to follow their example.

Love as a Witness for Christ

Ultimately, the love we show within our families and extend to others serves as a witness for Christ. In Matthew 5:16 (KJV), Jesus encourages us, *"Let your light so shine before men, that they may see your good works, and glorify your Father which is in heaven."* When we love others selflessly and sacrificially, we reflect the love of Christ and draw people closer to Him.

This is why love is so central to God's design for families. It is not just a personal virtue; it is a spiritual mandate. When families operate in love, they fulfill their role as ambassadors of Christ, spreading His message of grace and redemption to a world in need.

A Reflection on Love's Impact

As I reflect on my own journey as a husband, father, and pastor, I am continually amazed by the power of love to transform lives. I've seen families reconciled after years of estrangement, communities healed through acts of kindness, and individuals drawn to Christ simply by witnessing the love of those around them.

Love is not always easy. It requires patience, forgiveness, and humility. But as 1 Peter 4:8 (KJV) reminds us, *"And above all things have fervent charity among yourselves: for charity shall cover the multitude of sins."* The effort is always worth it, for love is the greatest gift we can offer—both to our families and to the world.

Looking Ahead

In the next part of this chapter, we will explore how love, combined with faith and unity, creates a lasting legacy. Love is not just for the here and now; it is an eternal investment that shapes future generations and honors God's plan for families.

For now, I encourage you to think about ways your family can extend love beyond your home. How can you serve others, build community, and reflect God's love to the world around you? Remember, love is not meant to be confined—it is meant to be shared.

As we conclude this chapter on love, it's essential to understand that love within a family is not just a gift but a responsibility. God has entrusted families with the privilege of modeling His love to one another and to the world. This responsibility carries with it the potential to create a legacy of love that transcends generations.

The Eternal Impact of Love

The love we cultivate within our families has an eternal impact. In 1 Corinthians 13:13 (KJV), Paul writes, *"And now abideth faith, hope, charity, these three; but the greatest of these is charity."* Charity, or love, is the greatest because it is the essence of God Himself. When we love as God loves, we participate in His divine nature and contribute to His eternal kingdom.

Consider the legacy of love left by faithful families throughout history. Generations have been shaped by the prayers, sacrifices, and unwavering love of those who came before them. This is the power of family love—it doesn't end with us. It multiplies, influencing the lives of our children, grandchildren, and beyond.

Teaching Love Through Actions

Words are powerful, but actions often speak louder. Children learn what love looks like not just by hearing it but by seeing it lived out daily. James 2:17 (KJV) reminds us, *"Even so faith, if it hath not works, is dead, being alone."* Similarly, love without action is incomplete. Here are some ways to teach love through actions:

1. **Be Consistent**
   - Show love in both the big and small moments. A consistent demonstration of care and kindness creates a sense of security and trust within the family.

2. **Sacrifice When Needed**
   - Love often requires putting others' needs before your own. This could mean giving up personal time to support a family member or making financial sacrifices for the well-being of the household.

3. **Demonstrate Grace**
   - When mistakes are made, respond with understanding and forgiveness. Love covers flaws with grace, just as God covers our sins through His love.

4. **Celebrate Together**
   - Love finds joy in the successes of others. Celebrate milestones, achievements, and even small victories as a family. Romans 12:15 (KJV) encourages us to, *"Rejoice with them that do rejoice, and weep with them that weep."*

Love as a Generational Investment

Loving your family is not just about today; it's about preparing for tomorrow. Each act of love, no matter how small, is an investment in the future. Deuteronomy 6:6-7 (KJV) commands us, *"And these words, which I command thee this day, shall be in thine heart: And thou shalt teach them diligently unto thy children, and shalt talk of them when thou sittest in thine house, and when thou walkest by the way, and when thou liest down, and when thou risest up."*

This verse highlights the importance of passing down not only God's commandments but also His love. By teaching our children to love as God loves, we equip them to navigate life with compassion, humility, and strength.

One of my most cherished memories involves gathering with my grandchildren during the holidays. As we sit together, laughing and sharing stories, I am reminded that these moments of love and connection are far more valuable than any material possession. They are the threads that weave the fabric of our family's legacy.

A Family Built on Love Glorifies God

When families prioritize love, they glorify God. Ephesians 5:1-2 (KJV) exhorts us, *"Be ye therefore followers of God, as dear children; And walk in love, as Christ also hath loved us, and hath given himself for us an offering and a sacrifice to God for a sweet-smelling savour."* Walking in love means making it the foundation of every interaction, decision, and relationship within the family.

Families built on love reflect God's character to the world. They become a living testimony of His grace and goodness, drawing others toward Him. In this way, love fulfills its highest purpose—not just to bless the family but to glorify the One who is the source of all love.

A Prayer for Love in Your Family

As you reflect on the role of love in your home, I invite you to join me in this prayer:

Heavenly Father, thank You for the gift of love and the privilege of sharing it with our families. Help us to love as You love, with patience, kindness, and grace. May our homes be filled with Your presence and our relationships strengthened by Your Spirit. Let our love be a reflection of Your glory and a testimony to the world. In Jesus' name, Amen.

Looking Ahead

As we move into the next chapter, we will explore the foundational role of faith in building strong families. Faith is the anchor that keeps us grounded in life's storms, the guide that directs our steps, and the source of strength that enables us to love deeply and live purposefully.

But for now, let us commit to making love the cornerstone of our families. Remember, love never fails. It endures, it heals, and it transforms. Let it be the defining feature of your home and the legacy you leave for future generations.

Chapter 5: Faith as the Foundation of Family

The Role of Faith in God's Design for Family

God's design for family places faith at the center. From the very beginning, He established the family as a sacred institution meant to reflect His love, grace, and authority. In Joshua 24:15 (KJV), Joshua declared, *"But as for me and my house, we will serve the Lord."* This statement underscores the importance of a shared commitment to faith within the family unit.

Faith is not just an individual pursuit; it is a collective journey. When families embrace faith together, they create a foundation strong enough to withstand any challenge. This foundation is built through prayer, worship, and trust in God's promises.

Faith as an Anchor in Times of Trouble

Life is full of uncertainties. Financial struggles, health crises, and relational conflicts are all part of the human experience. But faith offers families a way to navigate these challenges with hope and confidence. Hebrews 11:1 (KJV) defines faith as, *"the substance of things hoped for, the evidence of things not seen."* It is the assurance that God is in control, even when circumstances seem bleak.

I recall a family in our congregation who faced a devastating loss— the sudden death of a loved one. The grief was overwhelming, and the temptation to despair was strong. But their faith in God became their anchor. Through prayer, scripture, and the support of their church community, they found comfort and strength. Over time, their sorrow gave way to peace, and they emerged from the trial with a deeper trust in God's faithfulness. Faith doesn't eliminate pain, but it provides the strength to endure it. It reminds us that our trials are temporary, and that God's promises are eternal.

Cultivating Faith as a Family

Building a foundation of faith requires intentional effort. Here are some practical ways families can cultivate faith together:

1. **Pray as a Family**

   - Prayer is the lifeline of faith. Set aside time each day to pray together, whether it's before meals, at bedtime, or during family devotions. Matthew 18:20 (KJV) assures us, *"For where two or three are gathered together in my name, there am I in the midst of them."*

     o Encourage each family member to share their prayer requests and participate in praying for others.

     o Use prayer as an opportunity to thank God for His blessings and seek His guidance.

2. **Study Scripture Together**

   - The Bible is the foundation of faith. Regularly reading and discussing scripture as a family helps everyone grow in their understanding of God's Word. Psalm 119:105 (KJV) reminds us, *"Thy word is a lamp unto my feet, and a light unto my path."*

   Choose a devotional or Bible reading plan that aligns with your family's needs and interests.

   Discuss what the scriptures mean and how they apply to your daily lives.

3. **Worship as a Family**

- Worship brings families closer to God and to one another. Attend church services together, sing hymns at home, or create a playlist of worship songs to enjoy as a family. Worshiping together reminds everyone of God's greatness and goodness.

4. **Live Out Your Faith**

- Faith is not just about belief; it's about action. Show your faith through acts of kindness, service, and generosity. James 2:17 (KJV) states, *"Even so faith, if it hath not works, is dead, being alone."* Model a faith that is active and alive, inspiring your family to do the same.

Passing Faith to the Next Generation

One of the greatest responsibilities of parents and guardians is to pass their faith on to the next generation. This involves more than teaching doctrines or attending church services; it requires living out a vibrant, authentic faith that children can see and emulate.

Deuteronomy 6:6-7 (KJV) provides clear guidance: *"And these words, which I command thee this day, shall be in thine heart: And thou shalt teach them diligently unto thy children, and shalt talk of them when thou sittest in thine house, and when thou walkest by the way, and when thou liest down, and when thou risest up."*

Children learn faith by observing how their parents respond to life's challenges, prioritize God's will, and treat others with love and compassion. When they see faith lived out consistently, they are more likely to embrace it as their own.

A Reflection on Faith's Role in My Family

Faith has been the cornerstone of our household. Valerie and I made a conscious decision early in our marriage to center our home on God's Word. This would require a determination to grow daily in the knowledge of his will. It requires devotion to God above each other. We knew inherently that God would do great things in our family if we did so. It wasn't always easy, especially during seasons of uncertainty or hardship. But each time we chose to trust God; He proved Himself faithful.

One memory stands out vividly. During a particularly challenging financial season, our natural inclination give up on the vision of ministry. But instead of letting fear take over, we gathered our children and prayed as a family. We asked God for provision, wisdom, and peace. That moment of collective faith not only strengthened our trust in God but also reinforced the bond within our family.

Looking back, I see how those moments of shared faith shaped our children. Today, as they navigate their own lives and raise their own families, they carry with them the lessons of faith we instilled.

Faith is not just a personal conviction; it is a generational gift. When families anchor themselves in faith, they create a legacy that impacts not only their children but also their grandchildren and beyond. This legacy is one of the most powerful ways we can honor God and fulfill His purpose for our lives.

The Generational Blessing of Faith

Throughout scripture, we see examples of faith passed from one generation to the next. Consider the faith of Abraham, which became the foundation for the covenant God established with his descendants. In Genesis 18:19 (KJV), God says of Abraham, *"For I know him, that he will command his children and his household after him, and they shall keep the way of the Lord, to do justice and judgment; that the Lord may bring upon Abraham that which he hath spoken of him."*

Abraham's faithfulness was not just for his benefit—it laid the groundwork for a nation. His example reminds us that our commitment to God extends beyond our own lives. It shapes the spiritual trajectory of those who come after us.

In my ministry, I've seen families transformed when one generation makes the decision to prioritize faith. Parents who choose to live according to God's Word often witness their children embrace the same values. This isn't to say the journey is always smooth or without challenges, but the foundation of faith provides a steadying influence that endures.

Faith as a Family's Compass

Life is full of choices, many of which have significant consequences. Without a clear sense of direction, families can easily become lost in the chaos of competing priorities and worldly distractions. Faith serves as a compass, pointing families toward God's will and helping them navigate the complexities of life.

Proverbs 3:5-6 (KJV) offers this wisdom: *"Trust in the Lord with all thine heart; and lean not unto thine own understanding. In all thy ways acknowledge him, and he shall direct thy paths."* When families place their trust in God, they invite His guidance and wisdom into their decisions.

I remember counseling a couple who were struggling to decide whether to move to a new city for a job opportunity. The decision carried significant implications for their family, and they felt torn between the promise of financial stability and the uncertainty of uprooting their lives. Through prayer and seeking God's will, they ultimately chose to prioritize what would best support their family's spiritual and emotional health. That decision, though challenging at the time, brought unexpected blessings and reinforced their reliance on God.

Practical Ways to Keep Faith Central

Keeping faith at the center of family life requires intentionality. Here are some practical steps to ensure your household remains rooted in God's Word:

1. **Make Time for Family Devotions**
   - Set aside regular time for family devotions, where you can read scripture, discuss its meaning, and pray together. Choose passages that address the needs and concerns of your family and encourage open dialogue.

2. **Celebrate Faith Milestones**
   - Recognize and celebrate spiritual milestones, such as baptisms, confirmations, or moments of answered prayer. These events serve as reminders of God's faithfulness and strengthen the family's bond.

3. **Speak of God's Faithfulness**
   - Share stories of how God has worked in your life. Whether it's a testimony of provision, healing, or guidance, these stories inspire faith and remind everyone of God's sovereignty.

4. **Keep the Sabbath Holy**
   - Prioritize regular worship as a family. Attending church together not only strengthens your faith but also provides an opportunity to connect with a broader community of believers.

Faith in Action: Serving Together

One of the most effective ways to deepen family faith is by serving others together. When families unite in acts of service, they demonstrate God's love and build a shared sense of purpose. Galatians 6:9-10 (KJV) encourages us, *"And let us not be weary in well doing: for in due season we shall reap, if we faint not. As we have therefore opportunity, let us do good unto all men, especially unto them who are of the household of faith."*

Serving together could mean volunteering at a local charity, participating in a church outreach program, or simply helping a neighbor in need. These experiences not only strengthen family bonds but also reinforce the importance of living out one's faith.

A Reflection on Faith in My Family

In our own family, faith has always been more than a concept; it has been the bedrock of our lives. I remember a season when one of our children faced a significant challenge that tested our faith. Valerie and I were deeply concerned but determined to trust God's plan. We prayed fervently, sought counsel, and supported our child with love and encouragement.

Looking back, I see how God used that experience to draw our family closer to Him. Not only did our child overcome the challenge, but we also grew stronger as a family. Our faith was refined, and our trust in God deepened.

A Call to Strengthen Your Family's Faith

As you reflect on your family's faith journey, consider these questions:

Is faith a visible and active part of your daily life?

Do your children see you seeking God's guidance in your decisions?

Are you modeling the kind of faith you hope to pass down to the next generation?

It's never too late to begin or strengthen your family's commitment to God. Start with small, intentional steps, and trust that He will honor your efforts.

Looking Ahead

As we continue this chapter, we will explore how faith not only sustains families but also equips them to fulfill God's purpose. Faith is the foundation of resilience, unity, and hope, enabling families to thrive even in the face of adversity.

For now, let faith be your family's compass, guiding your steps and illuminating your path. Remember, a family rooted in faith is a family prepared to face any challenge.

Faith is not merely a personal attribute; it is a powerful force that unites families and empowers them to fulfill God's purpose. A family rooted in faith becomes a beacon of hope, not only for its members but also for its community. As we continue to explore the role of faith, it is essential to recognize how it strengthens relationships, inspires resilience, and provides a sense of divine purpose.

Faith Strengthens Relationships

At its core, faith strengthens deeper connections between family members. When families are united by their shared belief in God, they develop a mutual understanding that transcends personal differences. Colossians 3:13-14 (KJV) encourages us, *"Forbearing one another, and forgiving one another, if any man have a quarrel against any: even as Christ forgave you, so also do ye. And above all these things put on charity, which is the bond of perfectness."*

This bond of love, strengthened by faith, allows families to approach disagreements with grace and resolve conflicts in a way that honors God. Faith provides a common framework for values, decision-making, and reconciliation, making it easier to navigate the inevitable challenges of family life.

I recall a family in our church who faced a period of intense conflict. Misunderstandings and unspoken grievances had created a rift that seemed insurmountable. However, when they chose to come together in prayer and seek God's guidance, their perspective shifted. Through their shared faith, they were able to forgive one another and rebuild their relationships. Today, their bond is stronger than ever, a testament to the healing power of faith.

Faith Inspires Resilience

Life's trials are inevitable, but faith equips families to endure and overcome them. James 1:2-3 (KJV) reminds us, *"My brethren, count it all joy when ye fall into divers temptations; Knowing this, that the trying of your faith worketh patience."* Faith transforms adversity into an opportunity for growth, teaching families to rely on God's strength rather than their own.

In my own family, there have been seasons when circumstances felt overwhelming. Financial challenges, health scares, and the pressures of ministry tested our resolve. But in those moments, faith became our anchor. We reminded ourselves of God's promises, such as Isaiah 41:10 (KJV): *"Fear thou not; for I am with thee: be not dismayed; for I am thy God: I will strengthen thee; yea, I will help thee; yea, I will uphold thee with the right hand of my righteousness."*

By trusting in God's provision and timing, we found the courage to face each challenge with hope and perseverance. These experiences not only strengthened our faith but also deepened our trust in one another.

Faith Provides a Sense of Purpose

Families rooted in faith understand that they are part of a larger story—God's story. This sense of divine purpose gives meaning to their actions and decisions, motivating them to live in a way that glorifies God. Ephesians 2:10 (KJV) reminds us, *"For we are his workmanship, created in Christ Jesus unto good works, which God hath before ordained that we should walk in them."*

When families embrace this purpose, they find joy in serving others, sharing the gospel, and supporting one another in their spiritual journeys. Faith becomes the driving force behind their actions, inspiring them to make a positive impact on the world.

I've seen this lived out through the ministry of Christian Families Against Destructive Decisions (CFADD). Families who commit to a God-first lifestyle often discover a renewed sense of purpose as they influence their communities and create legacies of faith. By prioritizing God's will, these families become vessels of His love and grace, inspiring others to follow their example.

Faith in Everyday Life

Faith is not confined to Sunday mornings or special occasions; it is meant to be a daily practice. Here are some practical ways to incorporate faith into your family's everyday life:

1. **Start the Day with Prayer**

   - Begin each day by praying together as a family. This sets a positive tone and reminds everyone to rely on God throughout the day.

2. **Speak God's Word**

   - Incorporate scripture into your conversations, using it as a guide for decision-making and encouragement. Deuteronomy 11:18-19 (KJV) emphasizes this: *"Therefore shall ye lay up these my words in your heart and in your soul, and bind them for a sign upon your hand, that they may be as frontlets between your eyes. And ye shall teach them your children, speaking of them when thou sittest in thine house, and when thou walkest by the way, when thou liest down, and when thou risest up."*

3. **Celebrate God's Blessings**

- Take time to acknowledge and give thanks for the blessings in your life, whether big or small. Gratitude strengthens faith and strengthens a spirit of joy.

4. **Model Faith in Action**

- Demonstrate your faith through acts of kindness, service, and integrity. Children and younger family members learn by example, so let them see your faith in action.

A Reflection on Faith's Transformative Power

Faith has the power to transform not only individual hearts but entire families. When families commit to living according to God's will, they experience a level of unity, strength, and purpose that cannot be achieved through human effort alone. Faith invites God into the center of family life, allowing Him to work in ways that exceed our expectations.

Faith is the family's strength and fortress. When families actively live out their faith, they create an environment of trust, hope, and spiritual resilience that equips them to navigate life's most difficult challenges. Let's delve deeper into how faith fortifies families, enabling them to thrive in every season of life.

Faith as a Source of Peace

In a world filled with uncertainty and chaos, faith brings peace that surpasses all understanding. Philippians 4:6-7 (KJV) reminds us, *"Be careful for nothing; but in every thing by prayer and supplication with thanksgiving let your requests be made known unto God. And the peace of God, which passeth all understanding, shall keep your hearts and minds through Christ Jesus."*

95

This peace is a gift that families can claim when they place their trust in God. It doesn't mean that life will be free of difficulties, but it does mean that even in the midst of trials, there is a sense of calm rooted in God's promises. Families who pray together and lean on their faith in challenging times experience this peace firsthand.

I remember a couple in our congregation who faced the uncertainty of a medical diagnosis for their young child. The fear and anxiety were overwhelming, but they chose to turn to God rather than let despair take hold. Through constant prayer, worship, and support from their faith community, they found peace in knowing that God was with them. Their unwavering faith not only sustained them but also inspired others who witnessed their journey.

Faith as a Shield Against Division

Families are often tested by external pressures—financial stress, societal expectations, and cultural shifts—that can drive wedges between members. Faith acts as a shield, protecting the family from division and discord. Ephesians 6:16 (KJV) speaks to this: *"Above all, taking the shield of faith, wherewith ye shall be able to quench all the fiery darts of the wicked."*

When faith is the central focus of a family, it creates a shared purpose and set of values that unite members, even in times of disagreement. Rather than succumbing to blame or frustration, families rooted in faith turn to God for guidance and strength. This unity not only strengthens relationships but also builds a legacy of cooperation and love.

Faith as a Catalyst for Growth

Faith doesn't just sustain families; it helps them grow. Romans 5:3-5 (KJV) tells us, *"And not only so, but we glory in tribulations also:*

knowing that tribulation worketh patience; And patience, experience; and experience, hope: And hope maketh not ashamed; because the love of God is shed abroad in our hearts by the Holy Ghost which is given unto us."

Every trial a family faces is an opportunity for growth. Faith transforms these moments into lessons, teaching patience, perseverance, and reliance on God. Families who approach challenges with this mindset often find themselves stronger and more united on the other side.

During times of difficulty, we've chosen to view challenges not as setbacks but as opportunities to deepen our faith and learn more about God's character. This perspective has allowed us to face life's uncertainties with hope and confidence, knowing that every trial serves a greater purpose in God's plan.

Living Faith Daily: Practical Applications

Faith must be lived out daily to truly transform a family. Here are some practical ways to make faith an active part of your family's life:

1. **Create a Family Prayer Routine**

   Dedicate time each day to pray together as a family. Whether it's in the morning, before meals, or at bedtime, this habit reinforces your reliance on God.

2. **Encourage Faith-Based Conversations**

   Discuss how your faith influences decisions, goals, and perspectives. Allow every family member to share their thoughts and questions about God and scripture.

3. **Participate in Faith-Building Activities**

   Attend church regularly, engage in Bible studies, and serve in ministry together. These activities strengthen your family's spiritual foundation and connect you with a community of believers.

4. **Model Faith During Challenges**

   Let your family see how you respond to difficulties with prayer, patience, and trust in God. Your example will teach them how to navigate their own challenges.

The Role of Community in Strengthening Faith

While faith begins at home, it is often strengthened within a community of believers. Hebrews 10:24-25 (KJV) emphasizes the importance of fellowship: *"And let us consider one another to provoke unto love and to good works: Not forsaking the assembling of ourselves together, as the manner of some is but exhorting one another: and so much the more, as ye see the day approaching."*

Families thrive when they are connected to a supportive church community. This connection provides encouragement, accountability, and resources that help families grow in their faith. It also creates opportunities for families to serve and contribute to the spiritual growth of others.

A Reflection on Faith's Power

Faith is a gift that God has given to every family. When we embrace it, nurture it, and live it out, it becomes a source of strength, unity, and joy. Families rooted in faith are not just prepared to endure life's storms—they are equipped to thrive, leaving a lasting impact on future generations.

Faith Empowers Families to Dream Boldly

Faith invites families to envision possibilities far beyond their immediate circumstances. Hebrews 11:6 (KJV) declares, *"But without faith it is impossible to please him: for he that cometh to God must believe that he is, and that he is a rewarder of them that diligently seek him."* Faith challenges families to dream in alignment with God's will, trusting that He can do exceedingly abundantly above all that we ask or think (Ephesians 3:20, KJV).

One of the most inspiring stories in scripture is that of Abraham. When God called him to leave his homeland and go to a place he had never seen, Abraham obeyed, trusting God's promise to make him the father of many nations. His faith not only shaped his family's destiny but also established a covenant that continues to bless generations.

In the same way, families today can trust God to guide them toward dreams and goals that align with His purposes. Whether it's pursuing a ministry, building a business, or simply raising children in the faith, God's plans are always greater than what we can achieve on our own.

Faith Gives Courage to Face Challenges

Faith equips families with the courage to face challenges and step into the unknown. Joshua 1:9 (KJV) offers this assurance: *"Have not I commanded thee? Be strong and of a good courage; be not afraid, neither be thou dismayed: for the Lord thy God is with thee whithersoever thou goest."*

In my own family, there have been moments when the road ahead seemed daunting. I remember a time when we were called to expand our ministry into a new community. The resources were limited, and the opposition was strong. Yet, through prayer and unwavering faith, we pressed forward, trusting that God would make a way. He did—and the fruits of that obedience continue to bless others to this day.

Families that rely on faith are not immune to fear, but they are empowered to move forward despite it. They draw strength from God's promises, knowing that He is with them every step of the way.

Faith Inspires a Legacy of Service

A family rooted in faith understands that its purpose extends beyond its own walls. Faith calls us to serve others, share the gospel, and contribute to the building of God's kingdom. Galatians 5:13 (KJV) reminds us, *"For, brethren, ye have been called unto liberty; only use not liberty for an occasion to the flesh, but by love serve one another."*

Families who embrace this calling often find that their acts of service bring them closer together. Serving as a family— whether through ministry, community outreach, or simple acts of kindness— creates shared memories and strengthens bonds. It also teaches children the importance of living out their faith in practical ways.

Living Faith Every Day

Faith is not a one-time decision but a daily commitment. Here are some ways families can ensure that faith remains an active part of their lives:

1. **Set Family Goals Rooted in Faith**
    - Discuss what your family hopes to accomplish, both spiritually and practically, and commit those goals to

God. Proverbs 16:3 (KJV) advises, *"Commit thy works unto the Lord, and thy thoughts shall be established."*

2. **Encourage Individual Growth**
   - While faith is a family journey, it is also deeply personal. Encourage each member to develop their own relationship with God through prayer, scripture, and reflection.

3. **Celebrate God's Faithfulness**
   - Regularly reflect on how God has worked in your family's life. Share testimonies of answered prayers and celebrate milestones of faith.

4. **Extend Grace and Forgiveness**
   - Just as God extends grace to us, families must practice grace and forgiveness with one another. This not only strengthens relationships but also reflects God's love.

A Legacy Built on Faith

As I reflect on the role of faith in my own family, I am reminded of the legacy it creates. Faith is not just for the present; it is an investment in the future. Deuteronomy 7:9 (KJV) declares, *"Know therefore that the Lord thy God, he is God, the faithful God, which keepeth covenant and mercy with them that love him and keep his commandments to a thousand generations."*

Each prayer, each act of service, and each step of obedience builds a foundation for future generations to stand upon. The choices we make today in faith will echo through our families for years to come.

Chapter 6: Unity as the Strength of Family

Unity is one of the most essential pillars of a strong and thriving family. It is the bond that holds a household together, enabling its members to face challenges with resilience, pursue goals with shared purpose, and cultivate relationships built on mutual respect and love. When families operate in unity, they reflect God's design and glorify Him through their harmony.

The Biblical Call to Unity

Scripture repeatedly emphasizes the importance of unity, not only in the church but also within families. Psalm 133:1 (KJV) declares, *"Behold, how good and how pleasant it is for brethren to dwell together in unity!"* This verse paints a picture of the joy and peace that come when families embrace togetherness.

Unity doesn't mean uniformity; it doesn't require every family member to think, act, or believe in exactly the same way.

Instead, unity celebrates diversity within a shared purpose. Just as the body of Christ is made up of many parts with different functions (1 Corinthians 12:12, KJV), so too are families composed of individuals with unique strengths and perspectives that contribute to the whole.

The Strength Found in Unity

When families are united, they can withstand the pressures and challenges that life inevitably brings. Ecclesiastes 4:12 (KJV) reminds us, *"And if one prevail against him, two shall withstand him; and a threefold cord is not quickly broken."* A unified family operates like a tightly woven cord, where each member supports the others, creating strength that is far greater than the sum of its parts.

I recall a family I counseled who faced a series of financial setbacks that threatened their stability. Instead of allowing the stress to drive them apart, they came together in prayer and worked as a team to find solutions. Each member contributed in their own way—whether through budgeting, taking on extra responsibilities, or offering emotional support. Their unity not only helped them overcome the crisis but also deepened their bond as a family.

Cultivating Unity Through Communication

One of the most effective ways to cultivate unity in a family is through open and honest communication. Ephesians 4:29 (KJV) instructs us, *"Let no corrupt communication proceed out of your mouth, but that which is good to the use of edifying, that it may minister grace unto the hearers."* Here are some principles for cultivating healthy communication within your family:

1. **Listen Actively**
   - Make an effort to truly hear what each family member is saying. Avoid interrupting or jumping to conclusions, and instead, seek to understand their perspective.

2. **Speak with Kindness**
   - Use words that build up rather than tear down. Even in moments of disagreement, choose a tone that reflects respect and love.

3. **Encourage Openness**

  - Create an environment where every family member feels safe to share their thoughts and feelings. This strengthens trust and prevents misunderstandings from festering.

4. **Resolve Conflicts Quickly**

  - Don't let disagreements linger. Address issues promptly and work together to find solutions. Matthew 5:9 (KJV) reminds us, *"Blessed are the peacemakers: for they shall be called the children of God."*

Unity in Purpose: Serving Together

Another way to strengthen unity is by pursuing shared goals and serving together as a family. When families align their efforts toward a common purpose, they create a sense of teamwork and mutual investment. Joshua 24:15 (KJV) famously states, *"As for me and my house, we will serve the Lord."*

Consider these practical ways to cultivate unity through shared purpose:

- **Set Family Goals**: Identify objectives that everyone can work toward, whether it's saving for a vacation, completing a home project, or supporting a charity.

- **Volunteer Together**: Serve your community or church as a family. Acts of service not only make a difference in the lives of others but also strengthen the bond between family members.

- **Celebrate Achievements**: Acknowledge and celebrate the milestones and successes that your family achieves together. This reinforces a sense of accomplishment and unity.

Overcoming Barriers to Unity

No family is perfect, and unity doesn't happen automatically. Barriers such as unresolved conflicts, misunderstandings, and selfishness can disrupt harmony within a household. However, these obstacles can be overcome through intentional effort and reliance on God's guidance.

1. **Practice Forgiveness**

    - Forgiveness is essential for maintaining unity. Colossians 3:13 (KJV) encourages us, *"Forbearing one another, and forgiving one another, if any man have a quarrel against any: even as Christ forgave you, so also do ye."* Letting go of grudges and extending grace paves the way for reconciliation and peace.

2. **Prioritize Time Together**

    - Busy schedules and competing priorities can pull families in different directions. Make an intentional effort to spend quality time together, whether through meals, activities, or family devotions.

3. **Seek God's Wisdom**

    - Pray for unity and ask God to reveal any areas where division may be taking root. James 1:5 (KJV) promises, *"If any of you lack wisdom, let him ask of God, that giveth to all men liberally, and upbraideth not; and it shall be given him."*

A Reflection on Unity in My Family

Unity has been a cornerstone of my own family's journey. Valerie and I have always made it a priority to cultivate an environment where every voice is heard, every need is considered, and every member feels valued. This hasn't always been easy—like any family, we've faced our share of conflicts and challenges. But by relying on God's Word and committing to open communication, we've been able to maintain a strong and unified household.

One of the most rewarding aspects of unity is watching it ripple out to future generations. When children grow up in a home marked by love, respect, and teamwork, they carry those values into their own relationships, perpetuating the cycle of unity.

Looking Ahead

In the next part of this chapter, we will delve deeper into the practical steps families can take to sustain unity over time. Unity is not a one-time achievement but a continual process of growth, effort, and reliance on God.

For now, reflect on the unity within your own family. Are there areas where division has taken root? What steps can you take today to strengthen greater harmony and togetherness? Remember, a family united in purpose and faith is a family equipped to glorify God in every aspect of life.

Unity within a family is both a gift and a discipline. It is something to be cherished but also something to be actively cultivated. In this section, we will explore practical steps families can take to strengthen their unity and deepen their connections, ensuring that the bonds they share remain strong and unshaken.

Unity Requires Intentionality

Unity does not happen by accident. It requires intentional effort from every family member. Amos 3:3 (KJV) asks a poignant question: *"Can two walk together, except they be agreed?"* Walking together as a family requires agreement—not in every opinion but in shared purpose and commitment.

Intentionality means making unity a priority. It means being willing to set aside individual desires for the good of the family. It also means actively seeking ways to nurture harmony and understanding.

Practical Steps to Cultivate Unity

1. **Establish a Family Mission Statement**

   - Just as organizations and ministries thrive when they have a clear mission, families benefit from having a shared sense of purpose. Sit down together and discuss your family's values, goals, and commitments. Write a mission statement that reflects your desire to honor God and support one another.

     For example: "Our family is committed to loving God, loving each other, and serving others with humility and grace."

2. **Create Traditions**

   - Traditions provide opportunities for families to come together and build lasting memories. These can be as simple as a weekly family game night, an annual holiday celebration, or a shared devotional time. Traditions create a sense of belonging and reinforce unity.

3. **Encourage Teamwork**

  - Families are strongest when every member
    contributes. Encourage teamwork by assigning
    responsibilities, working on projects together, or
    supporting one another's goals. Galatians 6:2 (KJV)
    exhorts us, *"Bear ye one another's burdens, and so
    fulfil the law of Christ."*

4. **Celebrate Differences**

  - Unity does not require uniformity. Recognize and
    celebrate the unique strengths, talents, and
    perspectives that each family member brings. Romans
    12:6 (KJV) reminds us, *"Having then gifts differing
    according to the grace that is given to us, whether
    prophecy, let us prophesy according to the proportion
    of faith."*

5. **Prioritize Forgiveness**

  - Unity cannot flourish where bitterness and resentment
    take root. Make forgiveness a cornerstone of your
    family's culture. Ephesians 4:31-32 (KJV) encourages
    us, *"Let all bitterness, and wrath, and anger, and
    clamour, and evil speaking, be put away from you,
    with all malice: And be ye kind one to another,
    tenderhearted, forgiving one another, even as God for
    Christ's sake hath forgiven you."*

Strength in Diversity

God designed families to be diverse. Each member has unique gifts,
personalities, and perspectives that contribute to the whole. This
diversity, when embraced, becomes a source of strength.

Consider the analogy of a garden. A garden filled with only one type of plant may look uniform, but it lacks the depth, beauty, and functionality of a garden with varied flowers, trees, and fruits. Similarly, families thrive when they recognize the value of their differences and learn to work together despite them.

1 Corinthians 12:12-14 (KJV) illustrates this beautifully: *"For as the body is one, and hath many members, and all the members of that one body, being many, are one body: so also is Christ. For by one Spirit are we all baptized into one body, whether we be Jews or Gentiles, whether we be bond or free; and have been all made to drink into one Spirit. For the body is not one member, but many."*

In my own family, I've seen how our differences have strengthened us. Some of us are natural problem-solvers, while others bring creativity or a calming presence. When we work together, each person's contributions make the whole stronger.

Overcoming Challenges to Unity

While unity is a goal worth striving for, it is not without its challenges. Families will inevitably face moments of conflict, misunderstanding, and tension. The key is to address these challenges head-on, with humility and grace.

1. **Address Conflicts Quickly**

   - When disagreements arise, don't let them linger. Matthew 18:15 (KJV) advises, *"Moreover if thy brother shall trespass against thee, go and tell him his fault between thee and him alone: if he shall hear thee, thou hast gained thy brother."* Approach conflicts with a spirit of reconciliation, seeking to restore rather than divide.

109

2. Pray Together

- Prayer is a powerful unifier. When families pray together, they invite God's presence and wisdom into their relationships. Philippians 4:6-7 (KJV) encourages us, *"Be careful for nothing; but in everything by prayer and supplication with thanksgiving let your requests be made known unto God. And the peace of God, which passeth all understanding, shall keep your hearts and minds through Christ Jesus."*

3. Seek Wise Counsel

- If a conflict feels insurmountable, don't hesitate to seek guidance from a trusted pastor, counselor, or mentor. Proverbs 11:14 (KJV) reminds us, *"Where no counsel is, the people fall: but in the multitude of counsellors there is safety."*

A Reflection on Unity's Importance

Unity is more than a practical necessity—it is a spiritual discipline. It reflects God's character and His desire for His people to live in harmony. Psalm 133:3 (KJV) compares unity to *"the dew of Hermon, and as the dew that descended upon the mountains of Zion: for there the Lord commanded the blessing, even life for evermore."* Unity brings blessing, life, and joy.

Generational Unity: A Lasting Legacy

The Bible emphasizes the importance of unity not just for the present but for the generations to come. Deuteronomy 6:6-7 (KJV) instructs, *"And these words, which I command thee this day, shall be in thine heart: And thou shalt teach them diligently unto thy children, and shalt talk of them when thou sittest in thine house, and when thou walkest by the way, and when thou liest down, and when thou risest up."*

When families prioritize unity, they model values, traditions, and faith that children carry forward into their own lives. This continuity creates stability and instills confidence in future generations. Grandparents, parents, and children all contribute to a legacy of love and cooperation that reflects God's design.

I've witnessed this in my own family. Watching my children raise their children with the same principles of faith and unity we instilled is one of the greatest blessings of my life. It is a reminder that the work we do today to build harmony within our homes has eternal significance.

Unity Builds Resilience in the Face of Adversity

Life's challenges are inevitable, but unity equips families to face them with strength and perseverance. Families that stand together are able to weather storms that might otherwise cause division or despair. Romans 8:28 (KJV) offers assurance: *"And we know that all things work together for good to them that love God, to them who are the called according to his purpose."*

Consider the example of the Israelites during their journey to the Promised Land. Though they faced numerous trials— hunger, thirst, and even internal conflicts—their shared purpose and reliance on God helped them persevere. Similarly, families that stay united through faith and mutual support can overcome even the most difficult circumstances.

One family in our church exemplified this principle during a season of financial hardship. Instead of allowing the stress to create division, they chose to work together. They established a budget, prayed as a family, and supported one another emotionally and practically. Through their unity, they not only overcame their financial challenges but also emerged stronger and more grateful for God's provision.

Unity Glorifies God

A family united in love and purpose is a powerful testimony of God's grace. John 13:35 (KJV) states, *"By this shall all men know that ye are my disciples, if ye have love one to another."* When families operate in unity, they reflect God's love and bring glory to His name.

Unity also enables families to fulfill their role as ambassadors of Christ. Whether through acts of service, hospitality, or evangelism, a united family can impact its community in profound ways. Their love and harmony serve as a light, drawing others toward God.

Practical Ways to Strengthen Generational Unity

1. **Create a Legacy of Faith**

   Share your family's faith journey with the next generation. Pass down stories of how God has worked in your life and encourage your children and grandchildren to cultivate their own relationships with Him.

2. **Establish Family Traditions**

   Traditions create a sense of continuity and belonging. Whether it's a weekly family meal, an annual trip, or a shared devotional time, these practices reinforce unity and strengthen bonds.

3. **Encourage Open Dialogue Across Generations**

   Strengthen communication between older and younger family members. Allow grandparents to share wisdom, parents to provide guidance, and children to express their thoughts and dreams.

4. **Serve Together**

   Engage in acts of service as a family. Whether it's volunteering at church, helping a neighbor, or participating in community outreach, serving together strengthens a sense of shared purpose.

Overcoming Barriers to Generational Unity

While generational unity is a worthy goal, it is not without challenges. Differences in perspective, communication styles, and life experiences can sometimes create misunderstandings. However, these barriers can be overcome with intentional effort:

1. **Practice Patience**
   - Unity takes time and effort. Be patient with one another, recognizing that understanding and harmony grow through consistent communication and mutual respect.

2. **Seek God's Guidance**
   - Pray for wisdom and discernment in navigating generational dynamics. James 1:5 (KJV) promises, *"If any of you lack wisdom, let him ask of God, that giveth to all men liberally, and upbraideth not; and it shall be given him."*

3. **Focus on Shared Values**
   - Emphasize the values that unite your family, such as faith, love, and respect. These shared principles provide a foundation for addressing differences and building unity.

A Reflection on Generational Impact

The greatest legacy we can leave is one of love and faith. The unity we cultivate today will shape the lives of those who come after us, creating a ripple effect that extends far beyond what we can see.

Unity is not just about the here and now; it is about eternity. Families united in Christ become part of His greater plan, contributing to the building of His kingdom and the fulfillment of His promises.

Unity Enables Families to Fulfill Their Calling

God has a unique plan and purpose for every family. Just as individuals are called to specific roles in God's kingdom, so too are families designed to carry out His work collectively. Ephesians 4:4-6 (KJV) emphasizes this shared calling: *"There is one body, and one Spirit, even as ye are called in one hope of your calling; One Lord, one faith, one baptism, One God and Father of all, who is above all, and through all, and in you all."*

When families operate in unity, they are better equipped to discern and pursue their God-given calling. This might involve ministry, community service, or simply being a light in their neighborhood. Whatever the calling, unity allows each family member to contribute their unique gifts and strengths toward a common purpose.

I have seen this principle in action through families who serve in our church. One family, in particular, stands out. Each member has a distinct role—one sings in the choir, another teaches Sunday school, while the parents lead a small group ministry. Their unity and shared commitment to serving God have not only strengthened their family but also blessed countless others in the congregation.

Unity Multiplies Impact

A family united in purpose can achieve far more than individuals working alone. Ecclesiastes 4:9 (KJV) reminds us, *"Two are better than one; because they have a good reward for their labour."* When families pool their resources, time, and talents, their impact is multiplied.

Consider the feeding of the five thousand (John 6:1-14, KJV). While the miracle was performed by Jesus, it began with the simple act of a young boy offering his loaves and fishes.

Imagine the ripple effect if every family approached their resources with the same willingness to serve. By working together, families can meet needs, solve problems, and inspire others to do the same.

Serving Together Strengthens Bonds

Serving others as a family not only blesses those around you but also strengthens the bonds within your home. Acts of service create shared experiences, strengthen teamwork, and instill a sense of

purpose. Galatians 5:13 (KJV) encourages, *"For, brethren, ye have been called unto liberty; only use not liberty for an occasion to the flesh, but by love serve one another."*

Here are some practical ways families can serve together:

1. **Volunteer in the Community**

   Look for opportunities to help in your neighborhood or local community. This could include serving at a food bank, cleaning a local park, or supporting a community event.

2. **Engage in Church Ministry**

   Join a ministry that allows your family to serve together. Whether it's welcoming visitors, participating in outreach programs, or supporting church operations, these efforts strengthen your family's unity and deepen your faith.

3. **Practice Hospitality**

   Open your home to others, offering meals, fellowship, or a listening ear. Hospitality is a powerful way to demonstrate God's love and create lasting connections.

Unity Reflects God's Glory

Ultimately, unity within a family glorifies God. When families operate in harmony, they reflect His love, grace, and design for humanity. John 17:21 (KJV) records Jesus' prayer for unity among His followers: *"That they all may be one; as thou, Father, art in me, and I in thee, that they also may be one in us: that the world may believe that thou hast sent me."*

This prayer underscores the importance of unity not only within the church but also within families. A family united in Christ serves as a living testimony of His presence, drawing others to Him through their example.

Overcoming Obstacles to Unity

While unity is a powerful force, it requires vigilance and effort to maintain. Families may encounter obstacles such as miscommunication, differing priorities, or external pressures. Addressing these challenges with humility and intentionality is key to preserving unity.

1. **Pray for Unity**

    - Prayer invites God to work in your family, revealing areas of division and providing the wisdom to address them. James 5:16 (KJV) reminds us, *"The effectual fervent prayer of a righteous man availeth much."*

2. **Establish Clear Communication**

    - Open and honest communication prevents misunderstandings and builds trust. Create a safe space where every family member feels heard and valued.

3. **Prioritize Reconciliation**

    - When conflicts arise, address them promptly and with a spirit of grace. Matthew 5:23-24 (KJV) teaches, *"Therefore if thou bring thy gift to the altar, and there rememberest that thy brother hath ought against thee; Leave there thy gift before the altar, and go thy way; first be reconciled to thy brother, and then come and offer thy gift."*

A Reflection on Unity's Eternal Value

Unity is not just about creating peace in the present; it is about building something that will last for eternity. Families united in Christ are part of His eternal kingdom, contributing to His redemptive plan for the world. As we strive for unity, we align ourselves with God's will and open the door for His blessings to flow through our lives.

Unity within families is more than a blessing, it is a responsibility. Families are called to model God's love and grace to one another, becoming examples of harmony and peace in a world often marked by division. Let us reflect on the transformative power of unity and consider how we can carry it forward in our homes and communities.

Unity Is a Daily Commitment

Unity is not a one-time achievement but a continual process that requires effort, grace, and reliance on God. Colossians 3:12-14 (KJV) provides a powerful reminder: *"Put on therefore, as the elect of God, holy and beloved, bowels of mercies, kindness, humbleness of mind, meekness, longsuffering; Forbearing one another, and forgiving one another, if any man have a quarrel against any: even as Christ forgave you, so also do ye. And above all these things put on charity, which is the bond of perfectness."*

Each day presents opportunities to practice unity through acts of kindness, words of encouragement, and choices that prioritize the family's collective well-being over individual preferences. It is in these small, consistent actions that unity takes root and flourishes.

Unity Strengthens Faith

A unified family is better equipped to grow in faith together. When family members support one another in their spiritual journeys, they create an environment where faith can thrive. This might include praying together, studying scripture, or encouraging one another to serve in ministry.

One family I know exemplifies this beautifully. Every morning, they begin their day with a shared devotional time. They read a passage of scripture, discuss its meaning, and pray for one another's needs. This practice has not only deepened their faith but also strengthened their bond as a family.

Unity in faith is especially powerful during times of trial. When challenges arise, a united family can lean on one another for support, reminding each other of God's promises and finding strength in their shared belief.

Unity Extends Beyond the Home

While unity begins within the family, its impact extends far beyond the walls of the home. A family that operates in harmony becomes a beacon of hope and love in its community.

Matthew 5:14-16 (KJV) reminds us, *"Ye are the light of the world. A city that is set on a hill cannot be hid. Neither do men light a candle, and put it under a bushel, but on a candlestick; and it giveth light unto all that are in the house. Let your light so shine before men, that they may see your good works, and glorify your Father which is in heaven."*

Families that practice unity become examples to others, showing what is possible when love and faith are prioritized. Their actions inspire neighbors, friends, and extended family members to seek the same harmony in their own lives.

Practical Steps to Maintain Unity

1. **Reflect Regularly on Your Family's Goals**
   - Take time to assess whether your family is moving in the same direction and working toward shared goals.

119

Adjust as needed to ensure alignment and purpose.

2. **Celebrate Achievements Together**
   - Acknowledge and celebrate the successes of individual family members and the family as a whole. These moments of joy reinforce the value of teamwork and shared purpose.

3. **Create a Culture of Gratitude**
   - Regularly express appreciation for one another. Gratitude strengthens a positive atmosphere and reminds everyone of the blessings they share.

4. **Pray for Unity**
   - Make unity a regular focus of your prayers, asking God to strengthen your family's bonds and guide you in resolving conflicts with grace.

A Reflection on Unity's Transformative Power

Unity transforms families by creating a foundation of love, trust, and purpose. It enables families to face life's challenges with resilience, pursue their calling with confidence, and leave a lasting legacy of faith. Most importantly, unity glorifies God, demonstrating His power to bring harmony and peace to a broken world.

As I reflect on my own family, I am reminded that unity has been one of our greatest sources of strength. It has allowed us to overcome obstacles, celebrate milestones, and grow closer to one another and to God. This unity did not happen by accident; it was built through prayer, intentional effort, and a shared commitment to God's will.

Chapter 7: Service as the Heart of Family

Service is the heartbeat of a thriving family. It is through acts of service that families demonstrate love, live out their faith, and reflect the character of Christ. Service is not just about giving; it is about embodying humility, selflessness, and compassion in everyday life. When families embrace a lifestyle of service, they strengthen their bonds, deepen their faith, and leave a lasting impact on the world around them.

The Biblical Call to Serve

Scripture is filled with examples of service and its importance in the life of a believer. Mark 10:45 (KJV) reminds us, *"For even the Son of man came not to be ministered unto, but to minister, and to give his life a ransom for many."* Jesus Himself modeled a life of service, consistently placing the needs of others before His own and teaching His followers to do the same.

Families that serve together reflect this Christ-like attitude. Service becomes a tangible expression of love—not only within the family but also toward neighbors, the church, and the broader community.

Service Strengthens Family Bonds

When families engage in service, they create shared experiences that strengthen unity and teamwork. These acts of giving and helping teach valuable lessons about empathy, gratitude, and the joy of making a difference. Proverbs 11:25 (KJV) states, *"The liberal soul shall be made fat: and he that watereth shall be watered also himself."* Serving others brings blessings not only to those receiving but also to those giving.

I've seen this firsthand through families in our church who volunteer together. Whether it's preparing meals for the homeless, cleaning the church sanctuary, or participating in outreach events, their service strengthens their relationships. They leave each experience more connected, with a renewed sense of purpose.

Practical Ways for Families to Serve

1. **Start Within Your Home**

   - Service begins at home. Encourage family members to look for ways to support one another through small acts of kindness, such as helping with chores, preparing meals, or offering encouragement during difficult times. Galatians 6:10 (KJV) instructs us, *"As we have therefore opportunity, let us do good unto all men, especially unto them who are of the household of faith."*

2. **Engage in Church Ministry**

   - Get involved in your local church. This might include volunteering in children's ministry, participating in the music team, or supporting hospitality efforts. Church service not only builds the community but also strengthens spiritual growth within the family.

3. **Reach Out to the Community**

   - Look for ways to serve your local community. This could involve visiting nursing homes, collecting donations for a food bank, or organizing a neighborhood clean-up. These acts of service create opportunities to share God's love with others.

Service Teaches Christ-Like Humility

Service requires humility—a willingness to place others' needs above one's own. Philippians 2:3-4 (KJV) exhorts us, *"Let nothing be done through strife or vainglory; but in lowliness of mind let each esteem other better than themselves. Look not every man on his own things, but every man also on the things of others."*

This humility is cultivated when families serve together, as they learn to prioritize the well-being of others and work collaboratively toward a common goal. Children, in particular, benefit from these lessons, as they grow to understand the value of compassion and selflessness.

Service Reflects God's Love

When families serve, they reflect God's unconditional love. Acts of service become a testimony of His grace and goodness, drawing others closer to Him. Matthew 25:40 (KJV) emphasizes this point: *"And the King shall answer and say unto them, Verily I say unto you, Inasmuch as ye have done it unto one of the least of these my brethren, ye have done it unto me."*

Every act of service, no matter how small, is significant in God's eyes. Whether it's offering a kind word, meeting a practical need, or simply being present for someone in need, these actions demonstrate His love in a tangible way.

A Reflection on Service in My Family

Service has always been a cornerstone of my family's devotion through faith. From a young age, Valerie and I taught our children the importance of giving back, whether through volunteering at church events or helping neighbors in need. These experiences not only enriched their understanding of God's love but also created a spirit of gratitude and generosity within our home.

At early ages our children participated in various ministries and outreaches assuming leadership as they matured. Ministries such as mentoring in Black Boys of Distinction a program I started in 2008, tutoring children of incarcerated parents, an opportunity I created for them. They have led community service projects, worship experiences as musicians and now are ordained elders and missionaries in our organization serving on a weekly basis in many areas.

Service Strengthens Spiritual Growth

When families commit to serving others, they often experience profound spiritual growth. Acts of service require stepping out of comfort zones, relying on God for strength and guidance, and prioritizing the needs of others. These experiences deepen faith and provide opportunities to see God's hand at work.

James 2:17 (KJV) reminds us, *"Even so faith, if it hath not works, is dead, being alone."* Service breathes life into faith, transforming belief into action. Families that serve together grow closer to God as they witness His presence in the lives they touch.

I recall a family in our congregation who felt called to serve in a local homeless shelter. At first, they were uncertain about how to approach the task. However, through prayer and perseverance, they discovered that their willingness to listen, encourage, and provide practical support was a powerful expression of God's love. This experience not only strengthened their faith but also inspired them to continue serving in new ways.

Service Cultivates Gratitude

One of the most remarkable outcomes of service is the way it cultivates gratitude. When families serve those in need, they gain a deeper appreciation for the blessings in their own lives. Philippians 4:12-13 (KJV) highlights this perspective: *"I know both how to be abased, and I know how to abound: everywhere and in all things, I am instructed both to be full and to be hungry, both to abound and to suffer need. I can do all things through Christ which strengtheneth me."*

Serving others reminds us that contentment is not found in material wealth but in the relationships and opportunities God provides. This shift in perspective is especially impactful for children, who learn to value what they have and develop a heart for giving.

Service Strengthens Family Bond

When families serve together, they create shared memories and deepen their connections. Service requires teamwork, communication, and mutual support—all of which strengthen relationships. Ecclesiastes 4:9-10 (KJV) states, *"Two are better than one; because they have a good reward for their labour. For if they fall, the one will lift up his fellow: but woe to him that is alone when he falleth; for he hath not another to help him up."*

Serving as a family strengthens a sense of unity and purpose. Whether it's organizing a community clean-up, volunteering at a church event, or simply helping a neighbor, these acts bring families closer together and reinforce the importance of working as a team.

The Transformative Power of Service

Practical Ways for Families to Serve in the Church and Community

1. **Adopt a Church Ministry Together**

   - Volunteer as a family in a church ministry that aligns with your strengths, such as greeting guests, serving in the nursery, helping with audiovisual production, or participating in the worship team. Encourage consistent involvement to model faithfulness.

2. **Host a Family Prayer Night**

   - Open your home for a regular prayer meeting or Bible study, inviting neighbors, church members, or other families. Lead the sessions together and foster spiritual growth in your community.

3. **Participate in Church Cleaning and Maintenance**

   - Dedicate time as a family to assist with cleaning, landscaping, or small repairs at your church. Take ownership of creating a welcoming and functional environment for worshippers.

4. **Organize a Church Outreach Event**

   - Work as a team to plan an event, such as a community meal, clothing drive, or youth activity, with your church. Each family member can contribute by handling specific tasks like setup, food preparation, or welcoming participants.

5. **Volunteer in Sunday School or Youth Programs**

   - Serve together by helping teach Sunday school, organizing youth group events, or mentoring teens.

Use your unique gifts to inspire the next generation of believers.

6. **Create Care Packages for Missionaries or Shut-ins**

   - Gather as a family to assemble care packages for missionaries supported by your church or for elderly members who can no longer attend services. Include handwritten notes, Scripture verses, and small gifts.

7. **Host a Fellowship Meal**

   - Use your home or church kitchen to host a meal after Sunday service or for special church events. Involve everyone in cooking, serving, and cleaning up as an act of hospitality.

8. **Support a New Family in the Church**

   - Partner with a recently joined family or a new believer, welcoming them with meals, helping them connect with others, or guiding them through church programs and resources.

9. **Lead a Seasonal Service Project**

   - Participate in seasonal outreach opportunities like Christmas gift drives, Easter events, or Thanksgiving meals for the less fortunate. Involve every family member in planning, execution, and follow-up.

10. **Maintain a "Family Mission Jar" for Church Needs**

    - Create a jar to collect spare change or small donations. Decide as a family how to use the funds to support church initiatives, such as contributing to a building project, sponsoring a missionary, or helping with benevolence requests.

11. Be a Hospitality Family

- Volunteer to host visiting pastors, missionaries, or guest speakers during their stay. Provide meals, accommodation, or transportation as needed, modeling generosity and service.

12. Start a "Family Mission Day"

- Dedicate one day each month to serving as a family in a church or community project, such as helping in a food pantry, leading a worship session at a nursing home, or distributing tracts and invitations.

13. Use Your Family's Talents to Bless Others

- If your family is musically inclined, offer to perform during services or special events. If you're artistic, create banners or decorations for the church. Find creative ways to use your gifts for ministry.

14. Pray for Church Leaders and Members

- Make a list of church leaders, missionaries, and families in need. Spend time as a family praying for their specific requests and send them notes of encouragement to let them know they are supported.

15. Mentor Another Family

- Partner with a family newer to faith or struggling in certain areas. Share meals, study Scripture together, and provide emotional and spiritual support.

These ideas emphasize teamwork and encourage every family member to participate, creating a strong sense of unity and purpose while serving others.

Service has the power to transform not only those who receive but also those who give. Acts 20:35 (KJV) reminds us, *"I have shewed you all things, how that so labouring ye ought to support the weak, and to remember the words of the Lord Jesus, how he said, It is more blessed to give than to receive."*

Through service, families learn to see the world through God's eyes. They develop compassion for others, a heart for justice, and a willingness to be His hands and feet. This transformation extends beyond individual households, creating ripples of kindness and love that impact entire communities.

Service Equips Families for God's Mission

God calls families to be active participants in His redemptive plan. In Matthew 28:19-20 (KJV), Jesus commands, *"Go ye therefore, and teach all nations, baptizing them in the name of the Father, and of the Son, and of the Holy Ghost: Teaching them to observe all things whatsoever I have commanded you: and, lo, I am with you alway, even unto the end of the world. Amen."*

This Great Commission is not limited to individuals—it extends to families. Through acts of service, families fulfill this mandate, sharing the gospel and meeting the physical and emotional needs of those around them. Whether it's through local outreach or global missions, families united in service become powerful ambassadors of Christ.

The Ripple Effect of Service

Service creates a ripple effect that touches countless lives. One act of kindness can inspire another, setting off a chain reaction of love and generosity. Galatians 6:9 (KJV) reminds us, *"And let us not be weary in well doing: for in due season, we shall reap, if we faint not."* Families that serve consistently sow seeds of hope, faith, and joy that bear fruit for generations.

I recall a family who began by volunteering at a local food bank. Their initial efforts seemed small—stacking shelves, distributing meals, and cleaning the facility. However, their consistency and compassion inspired others in the community to join them. Over time, what began as a single family's service transformed into a thriving outreach program that continues to bless hundreds of lives today.

Service as a Testimony of Faith

When families serve, they provide a living testimony of God's love and power. Acts of service demonstrate faith in action, showing others the tangible impact of a relationship with Christ. James 2:18 (KJV) states, *"Yea, a man may say, Thou hast faith, and I have works: shew me thy faith without thy works, and I will shew thee my faith by my works."*

Service also opens doors for meaningful conversations about faith. When people witness the selflessness and joy with which families serve, they often ask, "Why do you do this?" This question creates an opportunity to share the gospel, pointing others to the source of true hope and love.

Overcoming Barriers to Service

While service is deeply rewarding, it is not without challenges. Busy schedules, limited resources, and feelings of inadequacy can sometimes hinder families from stepping into opportunities to serve. However, these barriers can be overcome with intentionality and trust in God's provision.

1. **Start Small**
   - Service doesn't have to be elaborate to be impactful. Begin with small, manageable acts of kindness, such as writing encouraging notes or delivering meals to a neighbor. These simple gestures can grow into larger initiatives over time.

2. **Trust God for Resources**
   - If financial or time constraints make service feel daunting, remember that God is able to provide. Philippians 4:19 (KJV) assures us, *"But my God shall supply all your need according to his riches in glory by Christ Jesus."* Trust Him to multiply your efforts and meet every need.

3. **Involve the Whole Family**
   - Service is most effective when every family member participates. Assign roles based on individual strengths and interests, ensuring that everyone feels valued and included.

4. **Seek Community Support**
   - Partnering with other families, churches, or organizations can amplify your efforts and provide additional resources. Collaboration also strengthens a sense of unity and shared purpose.

The Eternal Impact of Service

One of the most beautiful aspects of service is its eternal significance. Acts of kindness and compassion may seem small in the moment, but their impact often extends far beyond what we can see. Matthew 25:21 (KJV) speaks of the reward awaiting faithful servants: *"His lord said unto him, Well done, thou good and faithful servant: thou hast been faithful over a few things, I will make thee ruler over many things: enter thou into the joy of thy lord."*

Every meal served, prayer offered, or hand extended in love contributes to God's kingdom. Families that serve with this eternal perspective find joy and fulfillment in knowing that their efforts are not in vain.

A Reflection on the Legacy of Service

Service creates a legacy that endures. Children who grow up witnessing and participating in acts of service are more likely to carry those values into their own lives, creating a ripple effect that spans generations. Proverbs 22:6 (KJV) reminds us, *"Train up a child in the way he should go: and when he is old, he will not depart from it."*

In my own family, service has been a thread that ties us together. Watching my children and grandchildren continue the traditions of giving and helping that we established fills me with gratitude and hope. It is a reminder that service is not just something we do—it is who we are as followers of Christ.

Sustaining a Lifestyle of Service

Sustaining service requires intentionality and a commitment to keeping God at the center. As Colossians 3:23-24 (KJV) reminds us, *"And whatsoever ye do, do it heartily, as to the Lord, and not unto men; Knowing that of the Lord ye shall receive the reward of the inheritance: for ye serve the Lord Christ."* Service is ultimately an act of worship, and maintaining this perspective helps families stay motivated and focused.

Practical Ways to Maintain a Service-Oriented Family Culture

1. **Make Service a Family Tradition**
   - Establish regular opportunities for service, such as volunteering at a soup kitchen during holidays or participating in annual church outreach events. These traditions become cherished memories and reinforce the importance of giving.

2. **Incorporate Service into Daily Life**
   - Service doesn't have to be reserved for special occasions. Look for ways to help others in your everyday interactions, whether it's offering to carry groceries for a neighbor, assisting a co-worker, or encouraging someone in need.

3. **Create a Vision Board for Service Goals**
   - As a family, brainstorm ways you want to make a difference and create a vision board to display your goals. This visual reminder keeps everyone inspired and focused on your mission.

4. **Celebrate Acts of Service**
   - Take time to acknowledge and celebrate the service efforts of each family member. Share stories of how your service has impacted others and reflect on the joy it brings to your family.

The Role of Gratitude in Service

Gratitude and service go hand in hand. When families approach service with a grateful heart, they are reminded of God's blessings and are inspired to share them with others.

1 Thessalonians 5:18 (KJV) encourages us, *"In everything give thanks: for this is the will of God in Christ Jesus concerning you."*

Tips for Cultivating Gratitude Through Service:

- **Keep a Family Gratitude Journal**

  Write down moments when you've seen God at work through your acts of service. Reflecting on these entries strengthens gratitude and reinforces the value of giving.

- **Pray Before and After Serving**

  Begin every act of service with a prayer of gratitude, thanking God for the opportunity to make a difference. Afterward, pray for those you've served and for the ongoing impact of your efforts.

- **Teach Children to Appreciate the Little Things**

  Help younger family members recognize God's provision in their lives. Encourage them to share how serving others has deepened their gratitude for their own blessings.

Service Brings Joy

One of the most profound truths about service is that it brings joy—not only to those who receive but also to those who give. Acts 20:35 (KJV) beautifully states, *"It is more blessed to give than to receive."* Families that serve together experience this joy firsthand, as they see the impact of their efforts and feel the fulfillment that comes from living in alignment with God's will.

I recall a family in our church who adopted a service project of visiting nursing homes. Initially, they were unsure of how their visits would be received. However, as they spent time listening to residents, singing hymns, and sharing scripture, they witnessed the joy their presence brought. Over time, these visits became a source of joy not only for the residents but also for the family, who cherished the connections they built.

Overcoming Service Fatigue

While service is deeply rewarding, it can sometimes feel overwhelming, especially when families take on significant commitments. It's important to recognize the signs of service fatigue and take steps to prevent burnout.

1. **Set Realistic Expectations**

   Understand your family's capacity and commit to projects that align with your abilities and time constraints. It's better to serve consistently in small ways than to overextend and risk burnout.

2. **Take Time to Rest**

   - Rest is a biblical principle and an essential part of sustaining service. Exodus 20:10 (KJV) instructs, *"But the seventh day is the sabbath of the Lord thy God: in it thou shalt not do any work."* Ensure that your family has time to recharge and reflect on your efforts.

3. **Seek God's Strength**

   - Service is not something we are meant to do in our own power. Philippians 4:13 (KJV) assures us, *"I can do all things through Christ which strengtheneth me."* Lean on God for strength and guidance when challenges arise.

A Reflection on Service's Impact

Service has taught me humility, strengthened my faith, and allowed me to witness God's love in action. It has also been a source of immense joy and fulfillment, reminding me that true greatness lies in serving others.

In my family, service has been a foundation upon which we've built our values and strengthened our relationships. Whether through church outreach, community projects, or simple acts of kindness, serving together has drawn us closer to one another and to God.

The Eternal Legacy of Service

Service is not confined to the moment; it creates ripple effects that last for generations. Families who prioritize serving others plant seeds of faith, love, and kindness that bear fruit long after their acts of service are complete. Proverbs 11:30 (KJV) reminds us, *"The fruit of the righteous is a tree of life; and he that winneth souls is wise."* Every act of service contributes to a legacy that glorifies God and draws others closer to Him.

Consider the story of the Good Samaritan (Luke 10:30-37, KJV). His willingness to help a stranger not only saved a life but also provided a timeless example of selfless love. Families who embody this spirit of service inspire others to do the same, creating a culture of generosity and compassion.

Families who have made service a cornerstone of their lives increase family capital. One family, in particular, began by volunteering at a local shelter. Over time, their children grew to love serving others, eventually leading their own initiatives in their schools and communities. This legacy of service has become a defining feature of their family's identity, passed down to grandchildren and beyond.

Service as Worship

Service is not just an act of kindness; it is a form of worship. When families serve, they glorify God by reflecting His love and fulfilling His command to care for others. Matthew 25:40 (KJV) emphasizes this: *"And the King shall answer and say unto them, Verily I say unto you, In as much as ye have done it unto one of the least of these my brethren, ye have done it unto me."*

Viewing service as worship transforms the way families approach it. It shifts the focus from obligation to opportunity, from burden to blessing. Families come to see service not as something they have to do, but as a privilege that brings them closer to God and His purposes.

Practical Steps for Leaving a Legacy of Service

1. **Teach by Example**
   - Children learn best by observing their parents. Model a heart of service by consistently seeking ways to help others and involve your children in these acts whenever possible.

2. **Document Your Family's Service Journey**
   - Keep a journal or scrapbook of your family's service activities. Include photos, stories, and

reflections on the impact of your efforts. This serves as a tangible reminder of your family's commitment to serving God and others.

3. **Involve the Next Generation**

   - Encourage children and grandchildren to take ownership of service projects. Allow them to choose causes they're passionate about and guide them in developing plans to make a difference.

4. **Partner with Other Families**

   - Collaborating with other families in service projects strengthens a sense of community and amplifies the impact of your efforts. It also creates opportunities for fellowship and mutual encouragement.

The Reward of Faithful Service

While the true reward of service is the joy of glorifying God and helping others, scripture promises eternal blessings for those who serve faithfully. Galatians 6:9 (KJV) reminds us, *"And let us not be weary in well doing: for in due season, we shall reap, if we faint not."*

Families who embrace a lifestyle of service often experience blessings in unexpected ways. They grow closer as a unit, deepen their faith, and find fulfillment in knowing they are making a difference. These rewards, both temporal and eternal, are a testament to the goodness of God.

A Reflection on the Power of Service

As I reflect on the role of service in my own life and ministry, I am reminded of its transformative power. Service has not only shaped my family but also strengthened my faith and deepened my understanding of God's love. It has taught me that the greatest impact we can have is often found in the smallest acts of kindness.

In my family, service has been a unifying force. Whether through church outreach, community involvement, or simple acts of compassion, we have seen how serving together draws us closer to one another and to God. These experiences have left an indelible mark on our hearts, reminding us that service is not just something we do—it is who we are as followers of Christ.

Chapter 8: Building a Legacy of Faith, Love, and Service

A family's legacy is not determined by wealth, achievements, or accolades but by the values it instills, the relationships it nurtures, and the faith it passes on to future generations.

Building a legacy rooted in faith, love, and service is one of the most profound ways families can honor God and impact the world.

What Is a Legacy?

A legacy is the lasting influence that one generation leaves for the next. Proverbs 13:22 (KJV) states, *"A good man leaveth an inheritance to his children's children: and the wealth of the sinner is laid up for the just."* While this verse may speak to material inheritance, the greatest inheritance families can leave is spiritual— a foundation of faith and a pattern of Christ-like living.

When families intentionally build a legacy of faith, love, and service, they create a ripple effect that shapes future generations and glorifies God.

The Foundation of a Godly Legacy: Faith

Faith is the cornerstone of a lasting legacy. It provides the spiritual foundation upon which all other values are built. Deuteronomy 6:5-7 (KJV) emphasizes this responsibility: *"And thou shalt love the Lord thy God with all thine heart, and with all thy soul, and with all thy might. And these words, which I command thee this day, shall be in thine heart: And thou shalt teach them diligently unto thy children, and shalt talk of them when thou sittest in thine house, and when thou walkest by the way, and when thou liest down, and when thou risest up."*

Teaching faith to the next generation involves more than words—it requires action. Families must model a life of trust in God, consistent prayer, and reliance on His Word. This lived example becomes a powerful testimony that children and grandchildren carry with them.

Practical Steps to Pass Down Faith:

1. **Create Regular Worship Practices**
   Establish family traditions such as daily devotions, regular church attendance, and scripture study. These routines provide consistency and reinforce the importance of faith.

2. **Share Testimonies of God's Faithfulness**
   Tell stories of how God has worked in your life. These personal testimonies make faith tangible and relatable for younger generations.

3. **Encourage Questions and Exploration**
   Create a safe space for children to ask questions about faith. Encourage them to seek answers in scripture and prayer, guiding them toward a deeper relationship with God.

The Power of Love in a Family's Legacy

Love binds the family together and enables them to leave a lasting impact. 1 Corinthians 13:13 (KJV) reminds us, *"And now abideth faith, hope, charity, these three; but the greatest of these is charity."* Love is both the motivation behind a family's actions and the measure of its success.

A legacy of love is built through daily acts of kindness, forgiveness, and encouragement. It is demonstrated in how family members treat one another and those outside the home. Families that prioritize love leave a legacy of warmth and unity that echoes through generations.

Practical Steps to Build a Legacy of Love:

1. **Practice Forgiveness**
   - Teach family members to resolve conflicts quickly and extend grace to one another. Colossians 3:13 (KJV) exhorts, *"Forbearing one another, and forgiving one another, if any man have a quarrel against any: even as Christ forgave you, so also do ye."*

2. **Celebrate Each Other**
   - Make it a habit to affirm and celebrate each family member's achievements and unique qualities. This strengthens a culture of encouragement and belonging.

3. **Extend Love to the Community**
   - Demonstrate love beyond your family by reaching out to neighbors, friends, and those in need. Acts of hospitality and kindness set an example for future generations.

Service as a Legacy Multiplier

Service amplifies the impact of faith and love, extending a family's legacy far beyond its immediate circle. Matthew 5:16 (KJV) reminds us, *"Let your light so shine before men, that they may see your good works, and glorify your Father which is in heaven."*

Families that embrace a lifestyle of service inspire others to do the same. Their commitment to helping others becomes a testimony of God's love and a source of inspiration for future generations.

Practical Steps to Cultivate a Legacy of Service:

1. **Mentor the Next Generation in Service**
   - Involve children in service projects from a young age, teaching them the value of giving their time and resources to others.

2. **Collaborate as a Family**
   - Work together on service initiatives, whether through church outreach, community programs, or simple acts of kindness. These shared experiences create lasting memories and instill a spirit of giving.

3. **Celebrate the Impact of Service**
   - Reflect on the difference your family's service has made and share stories of its impact. This reinforces the importance of service and motivates continued efforts.

A Reflection on Building a Legacy

Building a legacy of faith, love, and service requires intentionality and perseverance. It is not something that happens by chance but through daily choices to prioritize what matters most. Psalm 78:4 (KJV) captures this beautifully: *"We will not hide them from their children, shewing to the generation to come the praises of the Lord, and his strength, and his wonderful works that he hath done."*

As I reflect on my journey, I am reminded of the profound experience my parents and I shared when we dedicated our lives to serving the God of the Bible. Though my parents made this decision later in life, and I was already an adult, we experienced a radical rebirth within weeks of each other. This transformation established a legacy of faithfulness, love, and dedication to God's work, which my children have now inherited. It has also inspired them to build the same spiritual foundation for their own children and grandchildren. This legacy is not about material wealth or worldly success but about passing down a spiritual inheritance that honors God and blesses others.

Challenges to Building a Godly Legacy

Every family encounters challenges that threaten to derail its efforts to build a legacy of faith, love, and service. These obstacles may come in the form of external pressures, internal conflicts, or spiritual complacency. Recognizing these challenges is the first step toward addressing them effectively.

1. The Busyness of Life

Modern families are often overwhelmed by busy schedules, leaving little time for meaningful connection or spiritual growth. Activities such as work, school, sports, and social commitments can crowd out the priorities that matter most.

Solution:

Reclaim your time by setting clear priorities. Joshua 24:15 (KJV) declares, *"But as for me and my house, we will serve the Lord."* Make serving the Lord and building your family's legacy a central focus by carving out time for prayer, devotions, and family discussions. Establishing a rhythm of intentional connection ensures that faith, love, and service remain at the heart of your family's life.

2. Cultural Pressures

The world often promotes values that conflict with biblical principles, making it challenging for families to stay grounded in their faith. These cultural influences can create confusion, division, and distraction.

Solution:

Equip your family to stand firm in their faith by grounding them in scripture. Romans 12:2 (KJV) encourages, *"And be not conformed to this world: but be ye transformed by the renewing of your mind, that ye may prove what is that good, and acceptable, and perfect, will of God."* Regularly discuss God's Word as a family, addressing how it applies to the challenges you face in today's culture. Teach discernment and model Christ-like behavior in the face of worldly influences.

3. Generational Disconnect

Differences in perspectives, experiences, and communication styles can create barriers between generations, making it difficult to pass down values and traditions.

Solution:

Bridge the generational gap by cultivating open communication and mutual respect. Proverbs 20:29 (KJV) observes, *"The glory of young men is their strength: and the beauty of old men is the grey head."* Encourage grandparents, parents, and children to share their wisdom, experiences, and dreams. Create opportunities for mentorship, storytelling, and shared activities that bring generations together.

4. Spiritual Complacency

Over time, families may fall into routines that lack spiritual depth. Prayers become mechanical, devotions feel routine, and the spark of faith begins to dim.

Solution:

Reignite your family's passion for God by seeking fresh ways to engage in worship, study, and service. Revelation 2:4-5 (KJV) challenges believers to return to their first love: *"Nevertheless I have somewhat against thee, because thou hast left thy first love. Remember therefore from whence thou art fallen, and repent, and do the first works."* Attend a family retreat, explore new ministry opportunities, or embark on a mission trip to renew your sense of purpose and commitment.

Practical Strategies for Building a Legacy

Once challenges are addressed, families can focus on practical strategies to build and sustain their legacy. These steps ensure that faith, love, and service are woven into the fabric of daily life.

1. Establish a Family Mission Statement

A mission statement articulates your family's values and purpose, serving as a guide for decisions and priorities.

For example: "Our family is committed to glorifying God through faith, loving one another deeply, and serving others selflessly."

Display your mission statement prominently in your home and refer to it regularly as a reminder of your shared goals.

2. Create Traditions That Reflect Your Values

Traditions are a powerful way to reinforce faith, love, and service. Examples include:

- **Faith:** Weekly family devotionals, attending church together, or celebrating milestones such as baptisms and confirmations.
- **Love:** Annual family reunions, birthday celebrations, or writing letters of encouragement to one another.
- **Service:** Volunteering as a family during holidays, adopting a local cause, or participating in church outreach programs.

3. Celebrate Progress

Building a legacy is a long-term endeavor, but celebrating small victories along the way keeps families motivated. Whether it's completing a family service project, resolving a conflict with grace, or witnessing spiritual growth, take time to acknowledge and thank God for these moments.

The Role of Prayer in Building a Legacy

Prayer is the cornerstone of a godly legacy. It invites God's presence, guidance, and blessing into every aspect of family life. Philippians 4:6-7 (KJV) urges us, *"Be careful for nothing; but in everything by prayer and supplication with thanksgiving let your requests be made known unto God. And the peace of God, which passeth all understanding, shall keep your hearts and minds through Christ Jesus."*

Commit to praying together as a family, seeking God's wisdom for the legacy you are building. Pray for unity, faith, and opportunities to serve, and trust that He will guide your steps.

A Reflection on Perseverance

Building a legacy is not without its challenges, but it is a calling worth pursuing. Galatians 6:9 (KJV) reminds us, *"And let us not be weary in well doing: for in due season we shall reap, if we faint not."* Perseverance, rooted in faith and sustained by God's grace, ensures that your efforts bear fruit for generations to come.

As I reflect on the legacy my family has worked to build, I am reminded that it is a journey, not a destination. There have been moments of struggle and doubt, but through prayer, love, and service, we have seen God's faithfulness at every turn. This legacy is not about perfection; it is about pointing future generations to the One who is perfect.

Evaluating the Impact of Your Legacy

Periodically reflecting on the impact of your family's efforts is essential for staying on track. Proverbs 27:23 (KJV) advises, *"Be thou diligent to know the state of thy flocks, and look well to thy herds."* In the same way, families should take time to assess their spiritual, relational, and service-oriented goals.

Questions to Consider:

1. **Are We Growing in Faith?**
   - Do we consistently seek God's guidance in our decisions?
   - Are family members deepening their personal relationships with Christ?
   - Is faith an active part of our daily lives and conversations?

2. **Are We Demonstrating Love?**
   - Do we practice forgiveness, encouragement, and understanding with one another?
   - Are we creating an environment where each member feels valued and supported?
   - Do we extend love to others outside our home?

3. **Are We Committed to Service?**
   - Are we intentionally looking for ways to bless others?
   - Have we made service a regular part of our family's life?
   - Are we using our unique gifts and resources to glorify God through service?

Honest answers to these questions provide a clear picture of where your family is thriving and where adjustments may be needed.

Adapting to New Seasons

Life is marked by seasons, each bringing its own opportunities and challenges. Ecclesiastes 3:1 (KJV) reminds us, *"To everything there is a season, and a time to every purpose under the heaven."* Families must learn to adapt their legacy-building efforts to align with these changing seasons.

Examples of Adaptation:

1. **When Children Are Young:**
   - Focus on teaching foundational values through simple, hands-on activities such as Bible stories, family prayers, and age-appropriate service projects.

2. **During Adolescence:**
   - Encourage teenagers to take greater ownership of their faith, relationships, and service efforts. Provide guidance while allowing them to explore their unique interests and gifts.

3. **In Empty-Nest Years:**
   - Shift your focus to mentoring younger families, supporting community outreach, or deepening your involvement in ministry. Use your wisdom and experience to inspire others.

Staying Focused on God's Vision

In the busyness of life, it's easy to lose sight of the bigger picture. Isaiah 26:3 (KJV) offers reassurance: *"Thou wilt keep him in perfect peace, whose mind is stayed on thee: because he trusteth in thee.*" Staying focused on God's vision for your family requires intentionality and regular recalibration.

Practical Tips to Stay Focused:

1. **Schedule Regular Family Check-Ins**
   Set aside time each month to discuss your family's progress toward your spiritual, relational, and service goals. Use this time to pray together, celebrate successes, and address challenges.

2. **Keep Scripture at the Center**

   Let God's Word be your guide in every decision. Display key verses in your home, use them in family discussions, and apply them to your daily lives.

3. **Recommit to Your Mission Statement**

   Revisit your family's mission statement regularly to ensure that your actions align with your values. Adjust it as needed to reflect new goals or priorities.

4. **Celebrate God's Faithfulness**

   Take time to thank God for His blessings and provision. Acknowledging His faithfulness strengthens your family's trust in Him and reinforces your commitment to His purpose.

Inspiring the Next Generation

One of the most powerful ways to ensure the longevity of your legacy is by inspiring the next generation to carry it forward. Psalm 145:4 (KJV) declares, *"One generation shall praise thy works to another, and shall declare thy mighty acts."* Passing the torch requires intentional mentorship and encouragement.

Steps to Inspire Future Generations:

1. **Be Transparent About Your Journey:**

   Share the ups and downs of your family's faith, love, and service journey. Authenticity builds trust and makes your legacy relatable.

2. **Provide Opportunities for Leadership:**

   Encourage children and grandchildren to take initiative in family activities, service projects, and faith practices.

   Giving them responsibility strengthens confidence and ownership.

3. **Celebrate Their Contributions:**

   Affirm the unique ways each family member contributes to your legacy. Highlight their strengths and encourage them to use their gifts to honor God.

A Reflection on Staying the Course

Building a legacy of faith, love, and service is not without its challenges, but it is a calling worth pursuing. Galatians 6:9 (KJV) offers encouragement: *"And let us not be weary in well doing: for in due season we shall reap, if we faint not."* Perseverance, rooted in God's strength, ensures that your family's efforts bear fruit for generations to come.

As I reflect on my own journey, I am reminded of the importance of staying the course. There have been seasons of doubt, moments of struggle, and times when the path seemed unclear. Yet through it all, God has been faithful, guiding my family and affirming that the work we do for His kingdom is never in vain.

Celebrating Milestones Along the Way

Every step in building a legacy is an opportunity to celebrate God's faithfulness and the progress your family has made. These milestones serve as reminders of how far you've come and as encouragement to keep pressing forward. 1 Thessalonians 5:16- 18 (KJV) reminds us, *"Rejoice evermore. Pray without ceasing. In every thing give thanks: for this is the will of God in Christ Jesus concerning you."*

Ideas for Celebrating Milestones:

1. **Host a Family Gathering**

   - Mark significant moments, such as completing a service project, welcoming a new family member into faith, or overcoming a challenge together. Use these gatherings to reflect on God's blessings and share testimonies.

2. **Create a Legacy Scrapbook**

   - Document your family's journey with photos, written reflections, and keepsakes from service projects, family devotionals, and meaningful events. This visual record becomes a treasured reminder of your shared purpose.

3. **Establish Annual Traditions**

   - Dedicate a specific day each year to reflect on your family's values, revisit your mission statement, and set new goals. This tradition reinforces your commitment to building a lasting legacy.

4. **Give Thanks Together**

   - Set aside time for prayer and thanksgiving, acknowledging God's role in every success and milestone. As Psalm 107:1 (KJV) declares, *"O give thanks unto the Lord, for he is good: for his mercy endureth forever."*

The Joy of Seeing Lives Changed

One of the greatest rewards of building a legacy of faith, love, and service is witnessing the impact it has on others. When families live out their values, they inspire change not only within their home but also in their communities and beyond. Matthew 5:14-16 (KJV) reminds us, *"Ye are the light of the world. A city that is set on an hill cannot be hid. Neither do men light a candle, and put it under a bushel, but on a candlestick; and it giveth light unto all that are in the house. Let your light so shine before men, that they may see your good works, and glorify your Father which is in heaven."*

I've seen this firsthand through families who have made service a central part of their lives. One family began by volunteering at a local food pantry, unsure of the difference they could make.

Over time, their consistency and compassion inspired others in their community to join them. Today, their efforts have grown into a network of support that feeds hundreds of families each month. Seeing the lives changed by their legacy has deepened their joy and strengthened their faith.

Passing the Torch to Future Generations

A lasting legacy is one that endures through generations. Passing the torch requires intentional mentorship and a commitment to investing in the spiritual, emotional, and practical growth of younger family members. Psalm 78:6-7 (KJV) highlights this responsibility: *"That the generation to come might know them, even the children which should be born; who should arise and declare them to their children: That they might set their hope in God, and not forget the works of God, but keep his commandments."*

Practical Steps for Passing the Torch

1. Mentor with Intention

Spend time teaching younger family members about the values, traditions, and faith practices that define your legacy. Share personal stories of God's faithfulness and lessons learned along the way.

2. Encourage Leadership:

Give children and grandchildren opportunities to take the lead in family projects, devotionals, or acts of service. Guide them gently while allowing them to make decisions and learn through experience.

3. Model Perseverance

Demonstrate resilience and faithfulness in your own life, showing future generations how to navigate challenges while remaining committed to God's purpose.

4. Pray for Future Generations:

Cover your children, grandchildren, and great-grandchildren in prayer. Ask God to guide their paths, protect their hearts, and use their lives to glorify Him.

Leaving an Eternal Impact

A family legacy built on faith, love, and service has an impact that extends far beyond this life. It contributes to God's eternal kingdom, shaping lives and pointing others toward Him. Revelation 14:13 (KJV) provides comfort and assurance: *"And I heard a voice from heaven saying unto me, Write, Blessed are the dead which die in the Lord from henceforth: Yea, saith the Spirit, that they may rest from their labours; and their works do follow them."*

Every prayer offered, every act of kindness performed, and every soul reached for Christ contributes to a legacy that will endure forever. Families who embrace this truth find purpose and fulfillment in every step of their journey.

A Reflection on the Fruits of Legacy

As I reflect on my own journey, I am reminded of the countless moments when God has revealed the fruits of a life dedicated to faith, love, and service. Seeing my children raise their own families with the same values we instilled has been one of the greatest joys of my life. Knowing that our legacy will continue to impact future generations fills me with gratitude and hope.

Legacy is not about perfection; it is about faithfulness. It is about trusting that God will use our efforts, no matter how small, to accomplish His greater purpose.

As we draw closer to the conclusion of this chapter, it is crucial to understand that building a legacy of faith, love, and service is not a task limited to a single moment in time. It is an ongoing journey that requires steadfast commitment, humility, and trust in God's guidance. In this final section, we will explore how families can remain faithful to their legacy and persevere through the inevitable challenges they will face.

The Importance of Perseverance

Every meaningful legacy encounter challenges—moments when progress feels slow, obstacles seem insurmountable, or doubt creeps in. It is during these times that perseverance becomes essential. Galatians 6:9 (KJV) encourages us, *"And let us not be weary in well doing: for in due season, we shall reap, if we faint not."*

Families committed to building a lasting legacy must hold fast to their faith, trusting that their efforts are not in vain. Perseverance means continuing to pray, serve, and love, even when results are not immediately visible.

Strategies for Perseverance:

1. **Keep Your Eyes on the Goal**

   Remember why you began this journey. Reflect on your family's mission statement and the values that drive your efforts. Let the promise of leaving a godly legacy motivate you to press on.

2. **Encourage One Another**

   Families thrive when members lift one another up. Hebrews 10:24-25 (KJV) reminds us, *"And let us consider one another to provoke unto love and to good works: Not forsaking the assembling of ourselves together, as the manner of some is; but exhorting one another: and so much the more, as ye see the day approaching."* Celebrate small victories and offer words of encouragement during tough times.

3. **Trust in God's Timing**

   Building a legacy takes time, and the fruits of your efforts may not always be immediately evident. Ecclesiastes 3:11 (KJV) assures us, *"He hath made every thing beautiful in his time."* Trust that God is working, even when progress seems slow.

The Role of Faith in Sustaining a Legacy

Faith is the anchor that sustains families through every challenge. It is faith that allows families to see beyond present difficulties and trust in God's greater plan. Proverbs 3:5-6 (KJV) reminds us, *"Trust in the Lord with all thine heart; and lean not unto thine own understanding. In all thy ways acknowledge him, and he shall direct thy paths."*

Practical Ways to Strengthen Faith as a Family

1. **Regular Prayer**

   - Make prayer a cornerstone of your family's routine. Pray for wisdom, strength, and guidance as you navigate challenges together.

2. **Study God's Word**

   - Dedicate time to reading and discussing scripture as a family. Let God's promises provide comfort and direction during difficult seasons.

3. **Worship Together**

   - Attend church services and participate in worship as a family. This shared experience strengthens your spiritual connection and reinforces your commitment to God's purpose.

Remaining Rooted in Love

Love is the foundation of any lasting legacy. It is love that binds families together, motivates acts of service, and points others to Christ. Colossians 3:14 (KJV) declares, *"And above all these things put on charity, which is the bond of perfectness."*

When challenges arise, families must return to love as their guiding principle. Love is patient, kind, and forgiving, and it enables families to overcome obstacles while remaining united.

Practical Expressions of Love During Difficult Times:

1. **Show Grace**

   - When conflicts arise, approach them with compassion

and understanding. Extend forgiveness freely, just as Christ has forgiven us (Ephesians 4:32, KJV).

2. Serve One Another

- Acts of service within the family, such as helping with chores, offering emotional support, or simply listening, demonstrate love in action.

3. Speak Words of Affirmation

- Use your words to build each other up, especially during moments of doubt or discouragement. Proverbs 16:24 (KJV) states, *"Pleasant words are as an honeycomb, sweet to the soul, and health to the bones."*

Looking Beyond the Present

A godly legacy is not just about the here and now—it is about eternity. Families that remain steadfast in their commitment to faith, love, and service understand that their efforts contribute to something far greater than themselves. 1 Corinthians 15:58 (KJV) encourages, *"Therefore, my beloved brethren, be ye stedfast, unmovable, always abounding in the work of the Lord, forasmuch as ye know that your labour is not in vain in the Lord."*

This eternal perspective provides hope and motivation, reminding families that every prayer, every act of kindness, and every step of faith has significance in God's kingdom.

A Reflection on Faithfulness

As I reflect on the journey of building a legacy, I am reminded of the importance of remaining faithful in every season. There have been times when the road felt long and the challenges seemed overwhelming. Yet, through it all, God's grace has been sufficient. His faithfulness has strengthened my family and affirmed that every effort made in His name is worth it.

Legacy is not about perfection; it is about persistence. It is about trusting God to take our imperfect efforts and use them for His glory.

Sustaining the Legacy Through Continuous Growth

A legacy is not static—it requires ongoing growth and renewal. Families that remain open to learning, adapting, and deepening their faith will find that their legacy becomes stronger with each passing year. Philippians 3:13-14 (KJV) offers this encouragement: *"Brethren, I count not myself to have apprehended: but this one thing I do, forgetting those things which are behind, and reaching forth unto those things which are before, I press toward the mark for the prize of the high calling of God in Christ Jesus."*

Growth is a continuous process, and families must commit to pressing forward, even when the journey becomes challenging.

Ways to Strengthen Growth as a Family:

1. **Embrace Lifelong Learning**
   - Study scripture regularly, attend faith-building workshops or conferences, and seek out mentors who can guide your family in its spiritual journey.

2. **Reflect on Past Experiences**
   - Take time to review what has worked well and what

could be improved. Reflecting on both successes and challenges allows families to grow from their experiences.

3. **Set New Goals**

   • As seasons change, so do opportunities to serve and grow. Reevaluate your family's mission and set new goals that align with your evolving values and circumstances.

Leaving a Legacy Through Community Impact

A family's legacy is most evident in the way it impacts others. When families extend their faith, love, and service to the broader community, they create ripples that touch countless lives. Acts 1:8 (KJV) calls believers to this mission: *"But ye shall receive power, after that the Holy Ghost is come upon you: and ye shall be witnesses unto me both in Jerusalem, and in all Judaea, and in Samaria, and unto the uttermost part of the earth."*

Ways to Extend Your Legacy Beyond the Family:

1. **Mentor Other Families**

   Share your journey with others who may be starting their own path of building a legacy. Offer encouragement, resources, and practical advice to help them succeed.

2. **Engage in Local Outreach**

   Serve in your community through projects that meet real needs, such as feeding the hungry, mentoring youth, or supporting local ministries.

3. **Contribute to Global Missions**

   Partner with international organizations that share your values, providing financial support or participating in mission trips to spread God's love to the ends of the earth.

Celebrating God's Faithfulness

As families sustain their legacy, it is essential to celebrate God's faithfulness at every step of the journey. Psalm 100:4 (KJV) encourages us, *"Enter into his gates with thanksgiving, and into his courts with praise: be thankful unto him and bless his name."*

Celebrations remind families of God's provision, strengthen their bond, and inspire them to continue pressing forward.

Ideas for Celebrating God's Faithfulness:

1. **Host a Thanksgiving Service**

   Gather as a family to reflect on God's blessings, share testimonies, and offer prayers of gratitude.

2. **Create a Family Gratitude Journal**

   Record answered prayers, moments of joy, and acts of kindness that have marked your family's journey. This journal becomes a cherished record of God's goodness.

3. **Honor Milestones**

   Celebrate spiritual milestones such as baptisms, confirmations, or the completion of significant service projects. These moments reinforce the importance of your family's mission.

Faith, Love, and Service as an Eternal Legacy

The ultimate goal of building a legacy of faith, love, and service is not simply to create a better life for your family, but to glorify God and contribute to His eternal kingdom. Revelation 22:12 (KJV) offers a glimpse of the reward awaiting those who remain faithful: *"And, behold, I come quickly; and my reward is with me, to give every man according as his work shall be."*

Families that embrace this eternal perspective understand that their efforts have significance far beyond what they can see. They are part of a greater story—God's story—bringing hope, healing, and redemption to the world.

A Reflection on the Legacy We Leave Behind

As I reflect on the journey of building a legacy, I am filled with gratitude for the ways God has worked in my family and ministry. The seeds of faith, love, and service we have sown are not the result of our own efforts but of His grace and faithfulness. Knowing that this legacy will continue to bless future generations gives me peace and joy.

Each family has the opportunity to leave a legacy that reflects God's goodness and glorifies His name. This is not a calling reserved for a select few—it is a mission for all who follow Christ. By committing to faith, love, and service, families can create a lasting impact that endures through eternity.

Chapter 9: Overcoming Modern Challenges to Family Unity

In today's world, families face unprecedented challenges that threaten their unity and stability. From the pressures of technology and social media to the demands of busy schedules and cultural shifts, maintaining strong family bonds requires intentionality and resilience. Despite these challenges, families can overcome them through faith, love, and practical strategies rooted in biblical principles. This chapter will explore some of the most pressing modern challenges to family unity and offer guidance on how to address them effectively.

The 5 Greatest Challenges to Family Unity

Challenge 1: The Distraction of Technology

Technology has become a double-edged sword for families. While it offers convenience and opportunities for connection, it can also create significant distractions and barriers to communication. Devices that were designed to bring people together can, paradoxically, drive them apart, as family members become engrossed in their screens rather than engaging with one another.

Biblical Insight:

Psalm 46:10 (KJV) reminds us, *"Be still, and know that I am God."* In a world filled with constant notifications and digital noise, families must create space for stillness and genuine connection.

Practical Solutions:

1. **Establish Technology-Free Zones**

   Designate certain areas of your home, such as the dining room or living room, as spaces where devices are not allowed. This encourages face-to-face interaction.

2. **Set Limits on Screen Time**

   Create boundaries for how much time each family member can spend on devices. Use this time for shared activities, such as playing games, going for walks, or having meaningful conversations.

3. **Model Healthy Tech Habits**

   Parents should set an example by prioritizing family time over screen time. Demonstrate the importance of being present and engaged.

Challenge 2: The Pressure of Busy Schedules

Modern families are often stretched thin by work, school, extracurricular activities, and other commitments. These busy schedules can leave little time for meaningful connection, leading to feelings of disconnection and stress.

Biblical Insight:

Matthew 6:33 (KJV) reminds us to *"seek ye first the kingdom of God, and his righteousness; and all these things shall be added unto you."* Prioritizing God and family over the busyness of life is essential for maintaining unity.

Practical Solutions:

1. **Prioritize Family Time:**

   - Schedule regular family nights or meals where everyone comes together. Protect this time from outside commitments.

2. **Evaluate Activities:**

   - Periodically review your family's commitments and determine which activities align with your values. Be willing to say no to those that create unnecessary stress.

3. **Create Routines:**

   - Establish daily or weekly routines that strengthen connection, such as morning prayers, evening devotionals, or shared meals.

Challenge 3: Cultural Shifts and Conflicting Values

The rapid pace of cultural change has introduced values and norms that may conflict with biblical principles. Families often struggle to navigate these cultural pressures while staying true to their faith.

Biblical Insight:

Romans 12:2 (KJV) urges us, *"And be not conformed to this world: but be ye transformed by the renewing of your mind, that ye may prove what is that good, and acceptable, and perfect, will of God."* Families must be intentional about living out their faith in a culture that often pulls them in different directions.

Practical Solutions:

1. **Ground Your Family in Scripture:**

    *   Make God's Word the foundation of your family's values. Regularly read and discuss scripture together, applying its teachings to modern challenges.

2. **Have Open Conversations:**

    *   Create a safe space for family members to discuss cultural issues and how they relate to your faith. Encourage critical thinking and prayerful decision-making.

3. **Seek Community Support**

    *   Surround your family with like-minded believers who share your values. This support network provides encouragement and accountability.

Challenge 4: Generational Divides

Differences in perspectives, experiences, and communication styles can create friction between generations within a family. Bridging these divides is essential for maintaining unity.

Biblical Insight:

Proverbs 20:29 (KJV) observes, *"The glory of young men is their strength: and the beauty of old men is the grey head."* Each generation brings unique strengths and insights to the family, and these differences should be celebrated rather than viewed as obstacles.

Practical Solutions:

1. **Strengthen Mutual Respect**

   Encourage family members to value each other's perspectives. Teach younger generations to honor the wisdom of their elders while allowing older generations to appreciate the fresh ideas of youth.

2. **Create Opportunities for Collaboration**

   Plan activities or projects that require input and effort from all generations, such as service projects, family events, or creative pursuits.

3. **Encourage Storytelling**

   Invite older family members to share stories from their lives. This strengthens understanding, appreciation, and connection across generations.

Challenge 5: The Erosion of Communication

Effective communication is the foundation of family unity, yet it is often one of the first things to break down under stress or conflict. Misunderstandings, assumptions, and unspoken expectations can create barriers between family members.

Biblical Insight:

Ephesians 4:29 (KJV) instructs, *"Let no corrupt communication proceed out of your mouth, but that which is good to the use of edifying, that it may minister grace unto the hearers."* Families must strive to communicate in ways that build up rather than tear down.

Practical Solutions:

1. **Practice Active Listening**

   Give full attention to the speaker, making an effort to understand their perspective without interrupting or judging.

2. **Use "I" Statements**

   When addressing conflicts, express feelings and needs using "I" statements rather than accusatory language. For example, say, "I feel hurt when..." instead of "You always..."

3. **Schedule Check-Ins**

   Regularly set aside time to discuss how each family member is feeling and address any concerns. These check-ins strengthen trust and openness.

A Reflection on Overcoming Challenges

While the challenges facing families today may seem daunting, they are not insurmountable. With God's guidance and intentional effort, families can navigate these obstacles and emerge stronger, more united, and more grounded in their faith. Philippians 4:13 (KJV) provides reassurance: *"I can do all things through Christ which strengtheneth me."*

As I reflect on the challenges my own family has faced, I am reminded that each obstacle has been an opportunity to grow closer to one another and to God. The key has been staying anchored in His Word and prioritizing the relationships that matter most.

Building Resilience Through Faith

Resilience is the ability to bounce back from difficulties and grow stronger through them. For families, resilience is built on a foundation of faith and trust in God's sovereignty. Isaiah 41:10 (KJV) offers this assurance: *"Fear thou not; for I am with thee: be not dismayed; for I am thy God: I will strengthen thee; yea, I will help thee; yea, I will uphold thee with the right hand of my righteousness."*

Strategies for Cultivating Resilience:

1. **Strengthen Open Communication**

   Encourage family members to share their feelings and experiences during challenging times. Creating a safe space for expression builds trust and strengthens emotional bonds.

2. **Focus on Problem-Solving Together**

   Approach challenges as a team, brainstorming solutions and dividing responsibilities. This collaborative approach reinforces unity and demonstrates the power of working together.

3. **Lean on God's Promises**

   Regularly turn to scripture for encouragement and guidance. Memorize verses that remind your family of God's faithfulness and His ability to provide.

Finding Joy in the Midst of Challenges

Joy is not the absence of difficulty but the presence of hope and gratitude. Families that choose to focus on their blessings and maintain a positive perspective find that joy becomes a sustaining force even in the hardest times. Nehemiah 8:10 (KJV) proclaims, *"The joy of the Lord is your strength."*

Practical Ways to Increase Joy:

1. **Celebrate Small Wins**

   - Take time to acknowledge and celebrate even the smallest victories. Whether it's overcoming a minor obstacle or simply making it through a tough day, these moments of gratitude remind your family of God's goodness.

2. **Create Opportunities for Fun**

   - Engage in activities that bring laughter and connection, such as playing games, watching a family movie, or taking a walk together. These moments of lightheartedness renew energy and strengthen bonds.

3. **Practice Gratitude Daily**

   - Start or end each day by sharing something each family member is grateful for. This habit shifts focus from challenges to blessings and strengthens a culture of thankfulness.

Overcoming Financial Struggles

Financial stress is one of the most common challenges families face, often causing tension and division. However, by adopting a mindset of stewardship and relying on God's provision, families can navigate financial difficulties with wisdom and grace. Philippians 4:19 (KJV) reassures us, *"But my God shall supply all your need according to his riches in glory by Christ Jesus."*

Biblical Principles for Financial Stewardship:

1. Live Within Your Means

- Develop a family budget that prioritizes necessities and avoids unnecessary debt. Proverbs 21:20 (KJV) advises, *"There is treasure to be desired and oil in the dwelling of the wise; but a foolish man spendeth it up."*

2. Give Generously

- Even in times of scarcity, prioritize giving to others and to God's work. Luke 6:38 (KJV) promises, *"Give, and it shall be given unto you."* Generosity strengthens trust in God's provision.

3. Pray for Wisdom

- Seek God's guidance in financial decisions, asking for discernment and creativity in managing resources.

Strengthening Family Identity

One of the most powerful tools for overcoming challenges is a strong sense of family identity. Families that know who they are and what they stand for are better equipped to face difficulties with confidence and purpose. Joshua 24:15 (KJV) declares, *"But as for me and my house, we will serve the Lord."*

Steps to Reinforce Family Identity:

1. Clarify Core Values

Discuss and define your family's key values, such as faith, love, service, and integrity. Write these values down and display them as a reminder of what unites you.

2. **Create Shared Traditions**

   Establish routines and traditions that reinforce your family's identity, such as weekly devotionals, family meals, or annual service projects.

3. **Celebrate Your Unique Strengths**

   Recognize and affirm the unique talents and contributions each family member brings to the table. This strengthens a sense of belonging and mutual respect.

Staying Anchored in Prayer

Prayer is the cornerstone of overcoming challenges. Families that pray together draw strength from God and from one another, creating a spiritual foundation that sustains them through every trial. James 5:16 (KJV) reminds us, *"The effectual fervent prayer of a righteous man availeth much."*

Practical Ways to Make Prayer Central:

1. **Pray as a Family**

   Set aside time each day to pray together, lifting up your concerns, expressing gratitude, and seeking God's guidance.

2. **Encourage Individual Prayer**

   Teach each family member to develop a personal prayer life, emphasizing the importance of a direct relationship with God.

3. **Keep a Family Prayer Journal**

   Record prayer requests and answered prayers as a tangible reminder of God's faithfulness.

A Reflection on Resilience and Joy

As I reflect on the challenges my family has faced, I am reminded that resilience and joy are not products of our own strength but gifts from God. By leaning on Him, we have found the courage to persevere and the ability to rejoice even in the midst of trials. These experiences have deepened our faith and strengthened our unity, reminding us that God's grace is sufficient for every challenge.

Philippians 4:7 (KJV) beautifully captures this truth: *"And the peace of God, which passeth all understanding, shall keep your hearts and minds through Christ Jesus."*

Maintaining Hope in the Face of Adversity

Hope is a powerful force that sustains families during difficult times. It is rooted in the promises of God and provides the assurance that no challenge is too great for Him to handle. Romans 15:13 (KJV) reminds us, *"Now the God of hope fill you with all joy and peace in believing, that ye may abound in hope, through the power of the Holy Ghost."*

Practical Ways to Strengthen Hope:

1. **Focus on God's Promises**

   Regularly read and meditate on scriptures that highlight God's faithfulness and provision. Share these verses with one another to encourage hope and trust.

2. **Celebrate Progress**

   Acknowledge the steps your family is taking to overcome challenges. Celebrating even small victories reinforces the belief that God is working in your midst.

3. **Visualize a Positive Future**

   Discuss your family's goals and dreams, imagining how God will use your efforts to create a brighter tomorrow. This focus on the future provides motivation and inspiration.

Building Trust Within the Family

Trust is the bedrock of family unity. Without it, relationships falter, and misunderstandings grow. Trust is cultivated through consistent actions, open communication, and a commitment to prioritizing one another's well-being. Proverbs 3:5 (KJV) offers this timeless wisdom: *"Trust in the Lord with all thine heart; and lean not unto thine own understanding."*

Steps to Build Trust

1. **Be Consistent**

   Follow through on commitments and promises. Demonstrating reliability strengthens trust and shows that family members can depend on one another.

2. **Communicate Honestly**

   Practice transparency in your words and actions. Address concerns openly and listen without judgment to strengthen mutual respect.

3. **Show Empathy**

   Acknowledge each family member's feelings and perspectives. Empathy builds emotional safety and reinforces the bond of trust.

Handling External Influences

The outside world often introduces values, priorities, and pressures that conflict with biblical principles. Families must learn to filter these influences through the lens of their faith, choosing to align with God's truth rather than cultural trends. Psalm 119:105 (KJV) declares, *"Thy word is a lamp unto my feet, and a light unto my path."*

Strategies for Managing External Influences:

1. **Teach Critical Thinking**

   Encourage family members to evaluate media, conversations, and experiences against the teachings of scripture. This equips them to make decisions that honor God.

2. **Establish Boundaries**

   Set clear guidelines for what is acceptable in terms of media consumption, relationships, and activities. Boundaries provide protection and clarity.

3. **Strengthen Accountability**

   Create a culture where family members feel comfortable discussing challenges and seeking advice. Accountability strengthens unity and reinforces shared values.

Developing Spiritual Resilience

Spiritual resilience is the ability to maintain faith and trust in God during trials. It is a skill that families can cultivate together, ensuring that their unity is anchored in an unshakable foundation. Ephesians 6:10-11 (KJV) exhorts believers to *"be strong in the Lord, and in the power of his might. Put on the whole armour of God, that ye may be able to stand against the wiles of the devil."*

Practices for Building Spiritual Resilience:

1. **Engage in Family Worship**

   Dedicate time to worshiping God as a family through songs, prayer, and scripture. Worship strengthens spiritual bonds and invites God's presence into your home.

2. **Practice Spiritual Disciplines Together**

   Encourage fasting, prayer, and acts of service as a family. These disciplines deepen faith and create opportunities for spiritual growth.

3. **Seek God's Strength in Prayer**

   Turn to God during moments of doubt or fear, asking Him for the strength to persevere. Trust that He will equip your family for every challenge.

Increasing Joy in Everyday Life

Joy is a choice—a decision to focus on God's goodness and faithfulness rather than the difficulties of life. Families that cultivate joy find that it transforms their perspective, energizes their efforts, and strengthens their unity. Philippians 4:4 (KJV) commands, *"Rejoice in the Lord always: and again I say, Rejoice."*

Practical Ways to Cultivate Joy:

1. **Celebrate God's Blessings**

   Make it a habit to thank God for His provision, protection, and love. Sharing these moments of gratitude brings joy to your family's heart.

2. Create Opportunities for Fun

Plan activities that bring laughter and lightheartedness to your family life. These moments of joy provide relief and strengthen your bond.

3. Maintain a Positive Perspective

Focus on what is going well rather than dwelling on problems. Encourage one another with words of hope and affirmation.

A Reflection on Strength in Unity

As families face modern challenges, unity becomes both a goal and a source of strength. By cultivating hope, building trust, managing external influences, and cultivating joy, families can overcome even the most daunting obstacles. Ecclesiastes 4:12 (KJV) captures the power of unity: *"And if one prevail against him, two shall withstand him; and a threefold cord is not quickly broken."*

Moments of trial have not weakened us; they have drawn us closer, teaching us to trust, forgive, and persevere.

The Foundations of Unity

Unity begins with a shared purpose and a commitment to living out that purpose in every aspect of family life. Amos 3:3 (KJV) poses the question, *"Can two walk together, except they be agreed?"* For families, the answer lies in cultivating a clear sense of identity and aligning their actions with their values.

Steps to Establish Unity:

1. Define Your Family's Mission

- Collaboratively create a mission statement that outlines your family's core values and purpose.

This statement serves as a compass, guiding decisions and reinforcing unity.

2. **Commit to Shared Goals**

   - Work together to identify short-term and long-term goals that reflect your mission. Celebrate milestones along the way to keep motivation high.

3. **Embrace a Team Mentality**

   - View your family as a team, where each member contributes their unique strengths to achieve common objectives. This perspective strengthens collaboration and mutual respect.

Creating Rituals That Reinforce Unity

Rituals and traditions provide a sense of stability and belonging, reinforcing unity within the family. These practices serve as anchors, reminding family members of their shared values and priorities.

Examples of Unity-Building Rituals

1. **Family Meals**

   - Prioritize eating together as often as possible. Use this time to share stories, discuss the day's events, and strengthen emotional connections.

2. **Weekly Devotions**

   - Set aside time each week to study scripture, pray, and reflect on God's guidance as a family. This spiritual practice keeps God at the center of your unity.

3. **Annual Traditions**

   - Establish annual events, such as holiday
     celebrations, family vacations, or service projects,
     that bring everyone together and create lasting
     memories.

Maintaining Unity in the Face of Conflict

Conflict is inevitable in any family, but how it is handled determines
whether it strengthens or weakens unity. Ephesians 4:26-27 (KJV)
offers practical advice: *"Be ye angry, and sin not: let not the sun go
down upon your wrath: Neither give place to the devil."*

Strategies for Resolving Conflict:

1. **Prioritize Reconciliation**

   Address disagreements promptly and with a spirit of
   humility. Seek to understand the other person's perspective
   and work toward resolution.

2. **Establish Ground Rules for Disagreements**

   Agree as a family on how conflicts will be handled, such as
   speaking calmly, avoiding blame, and focusing on solutions.

3. **Pray Together**

   Invite God into moments of conflict, asking for wisdom,
   patience, and a spirit of forgiveness.

The Role of Gratitude in Building Unity

Gratitude is a powerful tool for cultivating unity. When family
members express appreciation for one another, it creates a positive
atmosphere that strengthens relationships and reduces tension.

Colossians 3:15 (KJV) encourages, *"And let the peace of God rule in your hearts, to the which also ye are called in one body; and be ye thankful."*

Ways to Practice Gratitude:

1. **Share Compliments Regularly**
   - Take time to acknowledge and affirm the contributions of each family member. This builds confidence and reinforces bonds.

2. **Keep a Family Gratitude Journal**
   - Record blessings, answered prayers, and moments of joy. Reflecting on these entries reminds everyone of God's goodness and the strength of your unity.

3. **Celebrate Achievements Together**
   - Recognize accomplishments, both big and small, as a family. Celebrations reinforce a sense of belonging and shared success.

Sustaining Unity Through Service

Service is not only a demonstration of love but also a powerful way to strengthen family unity. When families serve together, they develop a shared sense of purpose and deepen their connections with one another. Galatians 6:10 (KJV) reminds us, *"As we have therefore opportunity, let us do good unto all men, especially unto them who are of the household of faith."*

Ideas for Family Service:

1. **Community Outreach**
   Volunteer at a local shelter, food bank, or church ministry

as a family. These experiences create lasting memories and teach valuable lessons.

2. **Support Each Other's Goals**

    Look for ways to help family members achieve their personal aspirations, whether it's assisting with a school project, cheering at a sports event, or offering encouragement.

3. **Practice Everyday Acts of Kindness**

    Service doesn't have to be grand to be impactful. Simple acts, such as cooking a meal, helping with chores, or writing a note of encouragement, demonstrate love and unity.

A Reflection on Lasting Unity

As I reflect on the importance of family unity, I am reminded that it is both a gift and a responsibility. Unity is not something that happens by chance—it is the result of intentional effort, daily choices, and a reliance on God's grace. Families that prioritize unity find that it becomes a source of strength, joy, and resilience, enabling them to overcome challenges and glorify God.

Psalm 133:1 (KJV) beautifully captures the blessing of unity: *"Behold, how good and how pleasant it is for brethren to dwell together in unity!"* This verse reminds us that unity is not only desirable but also a reflection of God's design for families.

Prioritizing Time Together

In a world where schedules are packed and distractions abound, spending intentional time together is one of the most effective ways to strengthen family unity. Time is the currency of connection and investing it in your family reaps lasting rewards. Ecclesiastes 3:1 (KJV) reminds us, *"To every thing there is a season, and a time to every purpose under the heaven."*

Ways to Prioritize Time:

1. **Create Non-Negotiable Family Time**

   Set aside specific times each week when the entire family comes together, whether for meals, devotionals, or recreational activities.

2. **Engage in Meaningful Activities**

   Choose activities that strengthen conversation, teamwork, and laughter. This might include playing games, cooking together, or exploring nature.

3. **Be Fully Present**

   Put away devices and distractions during family time to ensure that everyone feels valued and heard.

Strengthening Unity Through Faith

Faith is the glue that holds families together during both joyful and challenging times. By placing God at the center of your family, you create a foundation that withstands the trials of life. Joshua 24:15 (KJV) declares, *"But as for me and my house, we will serve the Lord."*

Faith-Building Practices for Families:

1. **Start Each Day with Devotion**

   Begin your mornings with a short family prayer or scripture reading to set a spiritual tone for the day.

2. **Encourage Personal Faith Journeys**

   Support each family member in developing their personal relationship with God through prayer, Bible study, and involvement in ministry.

3. **Attend Church Together**

   Regular church attendance strengthens spiritual growth and provides a sense of community that reinforces family unity.

Embracing Forgiveness as a Cornerstone

No family is immune to misunderstandings, hurt feelings, or conflicts. However, forgiveness is the key to moving past these moments and restoring unity. Colossians 3:13 (KJV) instructs, *"Forbearing one another, and forgiving one another, if any man have a quarrel against any: even as Christ forgave you, so also do ye."*

Steps to Practice Forgiveness:

1. **Address Conflicts Quickly**

   Avoid letting anger fester by addressing disagreements as soon as possible. Seek resolution with humility and grace.

2. **Apologize and Accept Apologies**

   Teach family members to acknowledge their mistakes and ask for forgiveness. Equally important, encourage a spirit of grace and understanding when forgiving others.

3. **Learn from Each Experience**

   Use conflicts as opportunities for growth, discussing

what can be done differently in the future to prevent similar issues.

Encouraging Accountability

Accountability within the family strengthens a culture of trust, responsibility, and mutual respect. By holding each other accountable in love, families create an environment where everyone feels supported and empowered to grow.

Practical Ways to Strengthen Accountability:

1. **Set Family Goals**

   - Work together to establish goals related to spiritual growth, service, or relationships. Regularly check in on progress and celebrate achievements.

2. **Create a Safe Space for Feedback**

   - Encourage open, nonjudgmental conversations where family members can share constructive feedback and offer support.

3. **Model Accountability**

   - Parents should lead by example, demonstrating integrity, humility, and a willingness to accept feedback from their children.

Celebrating Unity

Celebrating unity reinforces its importance and strengthens the bonds between family members. These celebrations don't have to be elaborate; even simple acknowledgments of shared milestones and successes can have a profound impact. Psalm 126:3 (KJV) declares, *"The Lord hath done great things for us; whereof we are glad."*

Ideas for Celebrating Unity:

1. **Mark Special Occasions**

   Celebrate birthdays, anniversaries, and achievements with activities that bring the family together.

2. **Share Gratitude**

   During family gatherings, take turns expressing gratitude for one another and for God's blessings.

3. **Create Keepsakes**

   Document family moments through photos, journals, or scrapbooks that serve as reminders of your shared journey.

A Reflection on Unity's Eternal Value

Unity is not only a blessing for the present—it is an eternal investment. Families that prioritize unity reflect God's design and contribute to His kingdom by modeling love, forgiveness, and faithfulness. John 17:21 (KJV) records Jesus' prayer for His followers: *"That they all may be one; as thou, Father, art in me, and I in thee, that they also may be one in us: that the world may believe that thou hast sent me."*

This prayer underscores the divine significance of unity, not just within the church but also within families. By committing to unity, families become living testimonies of God's love and grace.

Chapter 10: Transforming Communities Through Family Capital

Strong families are the cornerstone of thriving churches and communities. When families embrace their God-given role as centers of love, faith, and service, they have the power to influence the world around them in profound ways. This chapter will explore how families can become agents of transformation in their communities, drawing from lessons learned through leading family ministries and the founding of Christian Families Against Destructive Decisions (CFADD). It will conclude with a call to action for families to invest in God- centered legacies that leave a lasting impact.

The Ripple Effect of Strong Families

When a family is grounded in faith, love, and service, its influence extends far beyond its own walls. The values cultivated within the home naturally flow into the church and the community, creating ripples of positive change. Proverbs 11:30 (KJV) declares, *"The fruit of the righteous is a tree of life; and he that winneth souls is wise."* A strong family is like a tree, its roots firmly planted in God's Word and its branches reaching out to bless others.

Impact on Churches:

Strong families strengthen the body of Christ by modeling unity, love, and service. They play vital roles in ministry, teaching future generations, and cultivating a culture of support and encouragement within the congregation. Families that actively serve together inspire others to do the same, creating a spirit of collaboration and purpose.

Impact on Communities:

In the broader community, strong families become beacons of hope. Their commitment to godly values challenges destructive cultural norms and provides a counterexample of stability, compassion, and generosity. Through acts of service, advocacy, and mentorship, these families meet tangible needs and point others to Christ.

Lessons Learned from Leading Family Ministries

Over the years, I have had the privilege of witnessing firsthand how strong families can transform churches and communities. Through my work in family ministries and the founding of CFADD, I have learned invaluable lessons about the power of family capital and the strategies that enable families to maximize their influence.

Lesson 1: The Family Is God's Design for Change

From the very beginning, God intended for the family to be the primary vehicle for passing down faith and shaping the moral fabric of society. Deuteronomy 6:6-7 (KJV) emphasizes the importance of teaching God's commandments to children: *"And these words, which I command thee this day, shall be in thine heart: And thou shalt teach them diligently unto thy children, and shalt talk of them when thou sittest in thine house, and when thou walkest by the way, and when thou liest down, and when thou risest up."*

Families that embrace this calling become catalysts for change, equipping future generations to live out their faith and impact the world.

Lesson 2: Leadership Begins at Home

Effective family ministry starts with personal commitment. I have learned that the most impactful families are those who prioritize their own spiritual growth and unity. As parents model faith, love, and service, their children naturally follow suit, creating a legacy of influence that extends beyond their immediate circle.

Lesson 3: Collaboration Multiplies Impact

Families do not have to act alone. By partnering with other families, churches, and organizations, their efforts are multiplied. CFADD has been a powerful example of this principle. By uniting families with a shared vision of promoting God-centered values, we have been able to address destructive decisions and strengthen stronger communities.

Lesson 4: Service Is the Bridge to Transformation

Service is one of the most effective ways for families to engage their communities. Whether through feeding the hungry, mentoring youth, or advocating for justice, acts of service demonstrate God's love in action and open doors for deeper relationships and spiritual conversations.

A Call to Action: Investing in God-Centered Legacies

As families, we have the unique opportunity to leave a legacy that honors God and transforms lives. This legacy is not built on wealth or accomplishments but on the values we pass down, the relationships we nurture, and the impact we make in our churches and communities.

Steps to Build a God-Centered Legacy:

1. **Prioritize Faith in Your Home**

   Make faith the foundation of your family's identity. Pray together, study scripture, and encourage one another in your spiritual journeys.

2. **Engage in Church Ministry**

   Actively participate in your church's mission by serving in ministries that align with your family's gifts and passions. Your involvement strengthens the body of Christ and inspires others to do the same.

3. **Serve Your Community Together**

   Look for opportunities to bless your community through acts of kindness, advocacy, and outreach. Service not only meets tangible needs but also reflects God's love to those who may not yet know Him.

4. **Mentor the Next Generation**

   Invest in younger families by sharing your experiences, offering guidance, and providing encouragement. This mentorship creates a ripple effect, empowering others to carry the torch of faith, love, and service.

5. **Partner with Organizations Like CFADD**

   Join movements that promote godly values and address the challenges facing families today. By working together, we can amplify our efforts and make a greater impact.

A Reflection on Family Capital's Transformative Power

As I reflect on my journey in family ministry and the founding of CFADD, I am continually amazed by the potential of strong families to transform their communities. Families that embrace their God-given role as agents of change become powerful testimonies of His grace and goodness. They demonstrate that the challenges facing our world—brokenness, division, and despair—can be overcome through faith, love, and intentional action.

Galatians 6:9 (KJV) offers encouragement for the work ahead: *"And let us not be weary in well doing: for in due season we shall reap, if we faint not."*

Strong families are not just essential for their own well-being; they are vital agents of transformation in the world around them. By embracing their role as God's ambassadors, families can influence their churches and communities in powerful and lasting ways. On this page, we will delve deeper into practical examples of how families can begin transforming their communities today and the role of collaboration in amplifying their impact.

Practical Ways Families Can Transform Communities

1. **Be a Light in Your Neighborhood**

   - Transformation often begins close to home. Families can start by building relationships with their neighbors, demonstrating kindness, and being available to help in times of need. Matthew 5:14-16 (KJV) reminds us, *"Ye are the light of the world. A city that is set on an hill cannot be hid."*

- **Examples:**
  - Host neighborhood gatherings or barbecues to strengthen community spirit.
  - Offer to help with practical needs, such as babysitting, yard work, or errands for elderly neighbors.
  - Share your faith naturally by living out your values and being open to conversations about God.

2. **Engage in Church-Led Initiatives**

   - Churches often serve as hubs for community outreach. Families that actively participate in these initiatives extend their influence beyond their immediate circles, joining hands with others to meet real needs.

   - **Examples:**
     - Volunteer at food banks, shelters, or clothing drives organized by your church.
     - Mentor younger church members, teaching them practical skills and spiritual lessons.
     - Lead or participate in prayer walks through your community, covering local needs in prayer.

3. **Support Local Schools**

   - Schools are often central to a community's well-being, and families can make a significant difference by partnering with educators and students.

- **Examples:**
  - o Volunteer as classroom aides, tutors, or mentors.
  - o Support school events and fundraisers, showing appreciation for teachers and staff.
  - o Advocate for programs that align with biblical values, such as character education or anti-bullying initiatives.

4. Advocate for Justice and Righteousness

- Families can serve as voices for truth and righteousness in their communities, standing against injustice and promoting values that reflect God's heart. Proverbs 31:8-9 (KJV) challenges us, *"Open thy mouth for the dumb in the cause of all such as are appointed to destruction. Open thy mouth, judge righteously, and plead the cause of the poor and needy."*

- **Examples:**
  - o Partner with organizations that combat human trafficking, poverty, or other injustices.
  - o Write letters or attend meetings to advocate for policies that protect families and uphold biblical values.
  - o Lead by example, teaching your children the importance of standing up for what is right.

The Role of Collaboration in Amplifying Impact

While individual families can make a difference, collaboration magnifies their efforts exponentially. Partnering with other families, churches, and organizations creates a network of support and resources, enabling families to tackle larger challenges and achieve greater results.

Benefits of Collaboration

1. **Shared Resources**

   Collaborating with others provides access to a wider range of skills, knowledge, and materials, making it easier to address complex issues.

2. **Encouragement and Accountability**

   Working alongside others strengthens a sense of community and mutual encouragement, helping families stay motivated and focused on their mission.

3. **Increased Reach**

   Partnerships allow families to extend their influence, reaching more people and addressing needs on a broader scale.

Examples of Collaborative Efforts:

- **Community Service Days**

  Partner with other families to organize a day of service, such as cleaning up parks, painting community spaces, or distributing care packages to those in need.

- **Family Ministry Networks**

  Join or create networks where families can share resources,

ideas, and support for strengthening their homes and communities.

- **Faith-Based Advocacy Groups**

   Work with like-minded organizations to advocate for policies and initiatives that align with biblical principles.

The Power of Family Ministries

One of the most effective ways to transform communities is by empowering families through ministry. CFADD, for example, has focused on equipping families to make God-honoring decisions and become leaders in their communities. By addressing issues such as destructive behaviors, broken relationships, and spiritual apathy, family ministries serve as catalysts for lasting change.

Lessons from CFADD's Approach:

1. **Education**

   Provide families with resources and training to address modern challenges, such as navigating technology, cultivating communication, and building financial stewardship.

2. **Mentorship**

   Pair experienced families with younger or struggling families to offer guidance, encouragement, and accountability.

3. **Community Engagement**

   Encourage families to take their values into the public sphere, influencing schools, workplaces, and local governments with the love and truth of Christ.

A Vision for Family-Led Transformation

Imagine a community where families are the heartbeat of positive change. Where parents and children work together to address needs, strengthen relationships, and glorify God in their actions. This vision is not only possible—it is what God desires for His people.

Isaiah 58:12 (KJV) beautifully captures this mission: *"And they that shall be of thee shall build the old waste places: thou shalt raise up the foundations of many generations; and thou shalt be called, The repairer of the breach, The restorer of paths to dwell in."*

Through faith, love, and service, families have the power to restore what is broken and build a foundation for future generations.

Creating a Sustainable Plan for Transformation

Sustainability is essential for lasting impact. Families must approach their efforts with a clear vision and a commitment to perseverance, ensuring that their actions remain effective and focused over time.

1. Define Your Family's Mission

Begin by crafting a mission statement that captures your family's values and goals for community transformation. Proverbs 29:18 (KJV) reminds us, *"Where there is no vision, the people perish."* A mission statement provides clarity and direction, ensuring that your efforts align with God's purpose.

Example Mission Statement:

"Our family is committed to glorifying God by serving our community, sharing His love, and building relationships that reflect His grace."

2. Identify Community Needs

Effective service begins with understanding the specific needs of your community. Take time to observe, research, and listen to those around you. Ask questions such as:

What challenges do our neighbors face?

How can we use our resources to meet these needs?

What unique gifts has God given our family to contribute?

Partnering with local organizations, churches, and community leaders can also provide valuable insights and opportunities for collaboration.

3. Set Realistic Goals

Break down your vision into achievable steps. Setting realistic goals ensures that your family remains motivated and avoids burnout. Consider both short-term and long-term objectives, and celebrate progress along the way.

Examples of Goals:

- **Short-Term:** Organize a neighborhood cleanup or deliver meals to families in need.
- **Long-Term:** Establish a mentorship program for local

youth or partner with other families to create a community garden.

4. Involve Every Family Member

Transformation is most effective when every family member contributes. Assign roles based on individual strengths and interests, ensuring that everyone feels valued and engaged.

Examples:

Younger children can write encouraging notes or help with simple tasks.

Teens can lead projects, such as organizing donation drives or teaching skills to peers.

Adults can provide guidance, resources, and logistical support.

5. Build Partnerships

Collaboration amplifies impact. Partnering with other families, churches, and community organizations enables you to pool resources, share ideas, and tackle larger challenges.

Examples:

Join forces with other families for a larger community service event.

Partner with a local church to provide after-school programs for children.

- Collaborate with nonprofit organizations to address systemic issues, such as homelessness or food insecurity.

Measuring the Impact of Your Efforts

While some aspects of community transformation are intangible, it is important to evaluate the effectiveness of your efforts. Measuring impact allows your family to reflect on what's working, make necessary adjustments, and celebrate the ways God is using you to make a difference.

1. Track Tangible Outcomes

Keep a record of the tangible results of your service, such as: The number of people served.

Resources distributed (e.g., meals, clothing, school supplies). Projects completed (e.g., playground renovations, community events).

2. Reflect on Personal Growth

Transformation begins within the family. Take time to discuss how your involvement in community service has impacted your relationships, faith, and personal growth.

Questions to Reflect On:

- How has serving others strengthened our family's unity?
- What lessons has God taught us through this experience?
- How have our actions deepened our faith and reliance on Him?

3. Seek Feedback

Invite feedback from those you serve and collaborate with. Their perspectives provide valuable insights into the effectiveness of your efforts and highlight areas for improvement.

Examples of Feedback Questions:

- What has been most helpful about our efforts?

- Are there additional needs we can address?

- How can we improve our approach?

4. Celebrate Successes

Recognizing and celebrating milestones reinforces the value of your efforts and motivates your family to continue. Whether it's a family dinner, a prayer of thanksgiving, or a shared moment of reflection, take time to acknowledge God's faithfulness and the impact He has enabled.

A Reflection on Faithful Service

As families commit to transforming their communities, it's important to remember that every act of service, no matter how small, carries eternal significance. Matthew 25:40 (KJV) reminds us, *"And the King shall answer and say unto them, Verily I say unto you, Inasmuch as ye have done it unto one of the least of these my brethren, ye have done it unto me."*

Transformation does not always happen immediately, but through faithful and consistent service, families can make a lasting difference. The seeds sown today will bear fruit for generations to come, glorifying God and blessing countless lives.

The Johnson Family: Advocates for Education

The Johnson family noticed a growing educational gap in their community, particularly among underprivileged youth. As a family, they decided to take action, pooling their resources and talents to launch an after-school tutoring program at their church.

- **Impact on the Church**

  The program quickly became a ministry of the church, attracting volunteers and providing opportunities for mentorship. The Johnsons also organized workshops for parents, equipping them to support their children's education.

- **Impact on the Community**
  Over the years, dozens of students have improved their grades, gained confidence, and pursued higher education.

  The Johnsons' efforts have inspired other families to start similar initiatives, multiplying the program's reach.

The Clark Family: Servants of the Marginalized

The Ramirez family felt called to serve the homeless population in their city. What began as monthly trips to distribute food and blankets evolved into a larger effort to connect people experiencing homelessness with resources for shelter, employment, and spiritual growth.

- **Impact on the Church**
  The Clarks partnered with churches to create a ministry dedicated to serving the homeless. Members of the congregation joined their efforts, offering donations, time, and prayer.

- **Impact on the Community**

  Through their work, the Clark family has helped countless individuals find hope and stability. Their consistent presence in the community has built trust and created opportunities to share the gospel.

The Fisher Family: Champions of Compassion

Living in a diverse neighborhood with a history of poverty, the Fisher family felt burdened to promote meet the needs of the underprivileged. They began hosting "community dinners," inviting people from all walks of life to share a meal and engage in open dialogue.

- **Impact on the Church**

  The Fishers' efforts bridged gaps between church members and their neighbors, creating an environment of inclusivity and understanding. Their pastor often uses these gatherings as opportunities to discuss faith and reconciliation.

- **Impact on the Community**

  The community dinners coupled with prison and nursing home ministry have strengthened friendships and enable many lives to be redeemed. What started as a simple act of hospitality has grown into a movement for evangelism.

The Inspiring Power of Family Action

These stories highlight a common truth: when families step out in faith to address needs, their actions have far-reaching effects. James 2:17 (KJV) reminds us, *"Even so faith, if it hath not works, is dead, being alone."* Faith in action not only changes lives but also glorifies God and draws others to Him.

Lessons from These Families

1. **Start Small**

   Each family began with a simple idea—a tutoring session, a meal, or a gathering. Small actions, when done consistently, lead to significant impact.

2. **Involve the Whole Family**

   By engaging every member of the family, these initiatives became shared missions that strengthened their bonds and multiplied their efforts.

3. **Trust God to Provide**

   None of these families had all the resources they needed when they began. Through prayer and faith, God provided the people, funds, and opportunities necessary to grow their efforts.

How Your Family Can Make a Difference

The examples above are not isolated instances—they are blueprints for how any family can make a difference. Whether your family feels called to address a specific need or simply wants to be more intentional about serving, God can use your unique talents and experiences to create change.

Steps to Begin

1. **Pray for Guidance**

   - Ask God to reveal the needs in your community and the role He wants your family to play.

2. **Start with Your Strengths**

   - Consider the skills, resources, and passions your

204

family already possesses. Use these as a foundation for your efforts.

3. **Partner with Others**
   - Collaborate with friends, church members, or community organizations to expand your reach and increase your impact.

A Reflection on Transformation

As I reflect on these stories and my own experiences with family ministry, I am reminded of the incredible potential within every family to create change. The families highlighted here did not wait for perfect conditions or endless resources—they simply took the first step in faith. Their stories are a testament to the truth of Ephesians 3:20 (KJV): *"Now unto him that is able to do exceeding abundantly above all that we ask or think, according to the power that worketh in us."*

Transformation begins with a willing heart and a commitment to follow God's leading. When families unite around a shared mission, their influence extends far beyond their own lives, creating ripples of hope and renewal in the world.

Establishing a Foundation for Long-Term Impact

Families that aim to transform their communities must begin with a solid foundation. This foundation includes clear goals, spiritual discipline, and a commitment to perseverance.

1. Set Long-Term Goals

Vision drives action. By establishing long-term goals, families can remain focused and motivated even when challenges arise.

Proverbs 16:3 (KJV) advises, *"Commit thy works unto the Lord, and thy thoughts shall be established."*

Examples of Long-Term Goals:

- Create a family ministry that mentors young couples or parents.

- Develop a program that addresses a specific community need, such as literacy, health, or employment.

- Raise funds or resources for ongoing projects, such as building a community center or supporting a missionary family.

2. Build a Culture of Prayer

Prayer is the cornerstone of sustained impact. Families that commit to regular, intentional prayer invite God's presence and guidance into their efforts.

Practical Ways to Incorporate Prayer:

- Begin each family meeting or project with prayer, seeking wisdom and unity.

- Keep a prayer journal to record requests, answers, and reflections.

- Pray specifically for the individuals and families you serve, asking God to work in their lives.

3. Develop a Support Network

No family can accomplish great things alone. Building a network of like-minded families, church members, and community organizations creates a framework for support, accountability, and collaboration.

Steps to Build a Support Network:

- Connect with other families who share your vision and invite them to partner with you.

- Establish regular check-ins or meetings to share progress, challenges, and ideas.

- Seek mentorship from leaders who have experience in ministry or community service.

Remaining Flexible and Open to Growth

As families engage in community transformation, they may encounter unexpected opportunities or challenges that require flexibility and creativity. Remaining open to growth ensures that their efforts remain effective and aligned with God's plan.

Be Willing to Adapt

Plans may change, and needs may evolve over time. Families must be willing to adjust their strategies while staying true to their mission.

Examples of Adaptation:

- Shifting focus from one project to another as community needs change.

- Incorporating new team members or volunteers to expand capacity.

- Exploring innovative ways to meet goals, such as leveraging technology or partnering with new organizations.

Celebrate Progress and Learn from Setbacks

Every milestone is an opportunity to celebrate God's faithfulness, while every setback offers a chance to learn and grow. Philippians 3:13-14 (KJV) reminds us, *"Forgetting those things which are behind, and reaching forth unto those things which are before, I press toward the mark for the prize of the high calling of God in Christ Jesus."*

Practical Steps:

- Host family or community celebrations to mark achievements.
- Reflect on challenges together, discussing lessons learned and adjustments needed.
- Reaffirm your commitment to the mission, trusting God to guide the path forward.

Passing the Torch to Future Generations

For community transformation to endure, families must actively invest in the next generation. By mentoring children, grandchildren, and other young families, they ensure that their legacy continues to grow.

Mentoring Future Leaders

Equip younger generations with the tools, values, and vision they need to carry the mission forward.

Ways to Mentor:

- Involve children in projects from an early age, teaching them the importance of service and leadership.

- Share stories of God's faithfulness and the impact of past efforts to inspire their commitment.

- Provide opportunities for youth to take on leadership roles within family or community initiatives.

Cultivating a Culture of Legacy

Encourage family members to see their efforts as part of a larger story—God's story of redemption and restoration. Psalm 78:6-7 (KJV) emphasizes this responsibility: *"That the generation to come might know them, even the children which should be born; who should arise and declare them to their children: That they might set their hope in God, and not forget the works of God, but keep his commandments."*

A Reflection on Sustained Transformation

As I reflect on the work of CFADD and other family ministries, I am reminded that true transformation takes time and perseverance. Families that remain committed to their mission, despite obstacles, become powerful instruments of God's love and grace. Their faithfulness not only impacts the present but also lays a foundation for future generations to build upon. Galatians 6:9 (KJV) offers encouragement for the journey: *"And let us not be weary in well doing: for in due season we shall reap, if we faint not."*

Chapter 11: Unleashing the Untapped Power of Family

Families are one of God's most profound gifts to humanity, designed to reflect His love, unity, and purpose. Throughout this book, we have explored the incredible potential of families to transform lives, communities, and generations. The untapped power of family lies in its ability to glorify God through faith, love, and service—a calling that each of us is equipped to embrace.

As we conclude, I want to leave you with a vision of what your family can achieve when fully surrendered to God's plan and an invitation to step boldly into this sacred mission.

The Power and Responsibility of Families

God created families to be the foundation of society, the first place where faith is taught, love is nurtured, and purpose is discovered. Families have the unique ability to influence generations, instilling values that shape character and inspire action. Psalm 78:5-6 (KJV) reminds us of this sacred responsibility: *"For he established a testimony in Jacob, and appointed a law in Israel, which he commanded our fathers, that they should make them known to their children: That the generation to come might know them, even the children which should be born; who should arise and declare them to their children."*

The Power of Families:

1. **To Shape Identity**
   - Families define who we are and guide us toward who we can become. By rooting their identity in Christ, families become unshakable in the face of challenges.

2. **To Demonstrate God's Love**

   - The love expressed within a family reflects the unconditional love of God. When families model forgiveness, patience, and sacrifice, they offer the world a glimpse of His character.

3. **To Create a Legacy**

   - Families have the power to influence generations, leaving a legacy of faith, hope, and love that endures long after they are gone.

The Responsibility of Families:

1. **To Glorify God**

   - Families exist not for their own sake but to bring glory to their Creator. Colossians 3:17 (KJV) declares, *"And whatsoever ye do in word or deed, do all in the name of the Lord Jesus, giving thanks to God and the Father by him."*

2. **To Serve Others**

   - Strong families look beyond themselves, seeking ways to bless their communities and share God's love with those in need.

3. **To Proclaim the Gospel:**

   - Families are called to be ambassadors of Christ, sharing the good news through their words, actions, and example.

A Personal Message to Readers

As I reflect on my own journey, I am reminded of the countless ways God has used families to transform lives, including my own. I have seen the power of a faithful family to inspire, heal, and lead others toward Christ. This is not because of our own strength or wisdom but because of the God who works through us.

To every reader: your family is part of God's plan. Whether you are just beginning your faith journey or seeking to strengthen your commitment, know that God has equipped you for this calling. The work of building a God-centered family is not always easy, but it is always worth it. Philippians 1:6 (KJV) assures us, *"Being confident of this very thing, that he which hath begun a good work in you will perform it until the day of Jesus Christ."*

To Begin Your Journey:

1. **Seek God Together**

   Start with prayer and scripture, inviting God to lead your family in this new chapter of faith.

2. **Prioritize Relationships**

   Focus on building strong, loving relationships within your family. Unity begins at home.

3. **Take the First Step**

   Whether it's committing to family devotions, serving your community, or addressing challenges with grace, take one step today to honor God within your family.

To Strengthen Your Journey:

1. **Reaffirm Your Commitment**

   Reflect on your family's mission and renew your dedication to living out God's purpose.

2. **Invest in Growth**

   Seek opportunities to grow spiritually, relationally, and in service to others.

3. **Share Your Faith**

   Let your family's story be a testimony of God's grace, inspiring others to follow Him.

Unleashing the Untapped Power

The power of family is a divine gift, one that holds the potential to change lives and glorify God in ways we cannot fully imagine. When families embrace this calling, they become beacons of hope in a world desperately in need of light. Joshua 24:15 (KJV) challenges us: *"As for me and my house, we will serve the Lord."*

I encourage you to make this declaration for your family today. Trust in God's plan, rely on His strength, and watch as He uses your family to accomplish extraordinary things. The untapped power of family is waiting to be unleashed, and its impact will echo into eternity.

A Final Prayer

Heavenly Father,

We thank You for the gift of family and the opportunity to glorify You through our lives. Help us to seek You first in all we do, to love one another as You have loved us, and to serve others with humility and grace. Strengthen us for the journey ahead, and may our families reflect Your light and truth to the world. We commit ourselves to Your purpose, trusting that You will guide us every step of the way. In Jesus' name, Amen.

A Closing Charge

The journey begins now. Embrace the power of family, take bold steps of faith, and trust that God will accomplish His good work through you. Together, let us unleash the untapped power of family for His glory and the good of His kingdom.

215

www.ingramcontent.com/pod-product-compliance
Lightning Source LLC
Chambersburg PA
CBHW060022100426

42740CB00010B/1567